UNIT 1: Sequence of the alphabet.
DIRECTIONS: Print the capital letters.
Print the small letters.

UNIT 1: Sequence of the alphabet.
DIRECTIONS: Print the letter that comes between the given letters.
Print the letters that come before and after the given letter.

a _____ c	_____ s _____
d _____ f	_____ d _____
t _____ v	_____ x _____
b _____ d	_____ e _____
f _____ h	_____ t _____
p _____ r	_____ o _____
m _____ o	_____ k _____

UNIT 1: Sequence of the alphabet.

UNIT 1: Sequence of the alphabet.
DIRECTIONS: Begin at ⊙ and follow the alphabet from dot to dot to form a letter. Find the letter, capital or small, in the words and draw a circle around it.

a b e f c · · d j · · l i k h g	Happy hello birthday surprise Here Mother
m n o p r q	look Little Hello milk Mother will
s t z y v u x w	Wants letters help Tom went Time

d e g h f m · · k l o n j i	something make rain Some Must Name
p q s t w · · r y x v u	Nuts know children farm new soon
u v x y w z	Live loves Vine every went ever

c	k m	s	q
k	p r	n	y
z	n p	o	p
y	d f	m	s
r	h j	g	b
b	s u	e	c
v	b d	h	n
i	r t	b	k
w	c e	x	d

a _____ f _____ k _ m

n _____ q _____ u _____ z

UNIT 1: Auditory recognition of beginning consonants.
DIRECTIONS: Print the capital and small letter with which the name of each picture begins. Color the pictures.

UNIT 1: Auditory recognition of ending consonants.
DIRECTIONS: Print the letter with which the name of the picture ends. Color the pictures.

to ___	we ___	su ___	be ___
pai ___	cu ___	do ___	ha ___
ha ___	lea ___	bo ___	dru ___

UNIT 1: Auditory recognition of ending consonants.
DIRECTIONS: Print the small letter with which the name of each picture ends.
Color the pictures.

UNIT 1: Auditory recognition of beginning consonants.
DIRECTIONS: Print the letter with which the name of the picture begins. Color the pictures.

___ ie	___ ig	___ ack	___ all
___ in	___ ap	___ esk	___ ive
___ am	___ ill	___ at	___ og

UNIT 1: Auditory recognition of beginning and ending consonants.
DIRECTIONS: Draw a red circle around the letter with which the name of each picture begins.
Draw a blue circle around the letter with which the name of each picture ends.

d p	f t	c d	c s
l r	b k	p b	d t
c x	p d	p g	g f
s k	b g	j b	l h
h t	q v	v m	b k
n r	w n	h n	t l

UNIT 1:   Auditory recognition of beginning and ending consonants.
DIRECTIONS: Say the name of the picture. If you hear the consonant at the beginning of the
word, draw a circle around the first consonant. If you hear it at the end of the
word, draw a circle around the last one.

UNIT 1: Auditory recognition of beginning and ending consonants.

DIRECTIONS: Say the name of the picture. Print the first and last letters you hear in the spaces below the picture.

UNIT 1:   Auditory recognition of middle consonants.
DIRECTIONS: What letter do you hear in the middle of the word? Print it below the picture.

UNIT 1: Auditory recognition of middle consonants.
DIRECTIONS: Say the name of the picture. What letter do you hear in the middle of the word?
Print the letter in the blank space in the middle of the word.

wa ___ on

Bill has a wa___on.

Color the wa___on red.

le___on

Can you see the le___on?

Color the le___on yellow.

pea___uts

Jack likes to eat pea___uts.

Color the pea___uts.

se___en

I can make a se___en.

Color the se___en green.

ru___er

Dad gave me a ru___er.

Color the ru___er blue.

coo___ies

Mother bakes coo___ies for me.

Color the coo___ies.

tu___ip

Here is a tu___ip.

Color the tu___ip red.

ca___el

The ca___el can eat grass.

Color the ca___el yellow.

13

UNIT 1: TEST: Auditory recognition of beginning, middle, and ending consonants.
DIRECTIONS: Say the name of the picture. In the blocks above each picture, print the beginning, middle, and ending consonants.

UNIT 2: Short vowel A.
DIRECTIONS: Draw a circle around the word that tells the name of the picture. Color all the
pictures.
If a word (or syllable) has only one vowel and it comes at the beginning or between
two consonants, that vowel is usually short.

hat	ham	bag	hat	camp	lad
hand	had	bat	bad	lap	lamp

sad	back	cat	cap	tam	jam
bag	bat	cab	can	Jack	am

wax	ax	mat	man	tag	tan
am	at	fan	tan	tap	tack

and	an	cat	can	mad	man
at	ant	cab	cap	map	mat

15

UNIT 2: Short vowel A in rhyming words.

DIRECTIONS: In each block, draw a circle around the word that does not rhyme. Draw a picture of what the word says.

cat		Max		cap	
fan		tax		tap	
hat		bag		map	
mat		wax		cab	
sack		bag		sand	
hand		rag		land	
back		cap		pan	
tack		tag		band	
ham		sad		quack	
fan		bat		cat	
ran		bad		sack	
can		had		back	
hand		pan		sat	
land		fan		ax	
lamp		Dan		pat	
sand		hat		fat	

UNIT 2: Short vowel A in rhyming words.
DIRECTIONS: Below each picture, print the name of the picture and a word that rhymes with it.
Do what the sentences tell you to do.

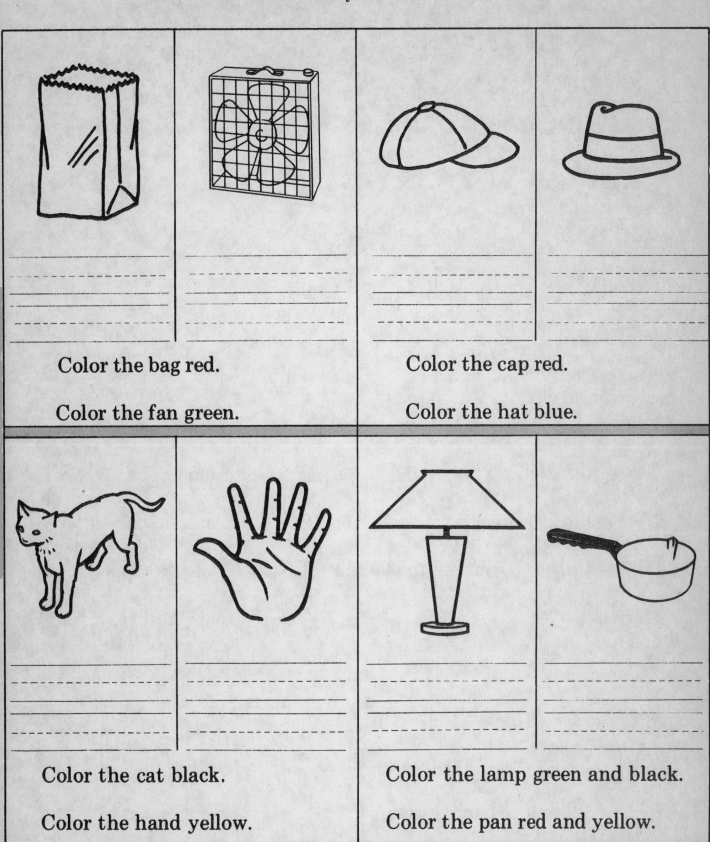

Color the bag red.

Color the fan green.

Color the cap red.

Color the hat blue.

Color the cat black.

Color the hand yellow.

Color the lamp green and black.

Color the pan red and yellow.

UNIT 2: Short vowel A.
DIRECTIONS: Draw a circle around the short A word that belongs in the sentence, and print it on the line.

1. Dad is a _____ .   band   man   sack

2. Pat ran to_____ .   Dad   and   fat

3. It is fun to go to _____ .   cat   lamp   camp

4. A little _____ is a kitten.   rat   cat   can

5. The boy can tip his_____ .   cab   cap   cat

6. The little duck said, "_____ ."   Back   Jack   Quack

7. Ann can not run as_____as Dan.   fan   fast   last

8. I will_____Mother if I may go.   as   ask   back

9. Next week I will play in a _____ .   land   band   bad

10. Here is the money for your _____ .   bank   bake   sat

11. _____went out to play with Bob.   Dan   Can   Ran

12. Mary has a red _____ .   nap   hat   fat

13. Dick_____to meet Father.   rap   fan   ran

14. Look_____Ann's little doll.   an   at   am

15. Come _____as fast as you can.   sat   quack   back

16. We _____fun at camp.   ham   lad   had

UNIT 2: Short vowel I.
DIRECTIONS: Draw a circle around the name of the picture. Color all the pictures.

silk milk mill bill	mitt bit fit mill	lid hid lip tip
tips lips dips dill	big pig fig pit	win tin will pin
mix six fix bit	bill bit hit bib	nk wink sink pink
hill bill sill mitt	Jig big Jill Jim	Bit Big Bill Hill

UNIT 2:   Short vowel I in rhyming words.
DIRECTIONS: Say the words in each ball. Color the parts of the ball which have rhyming words.

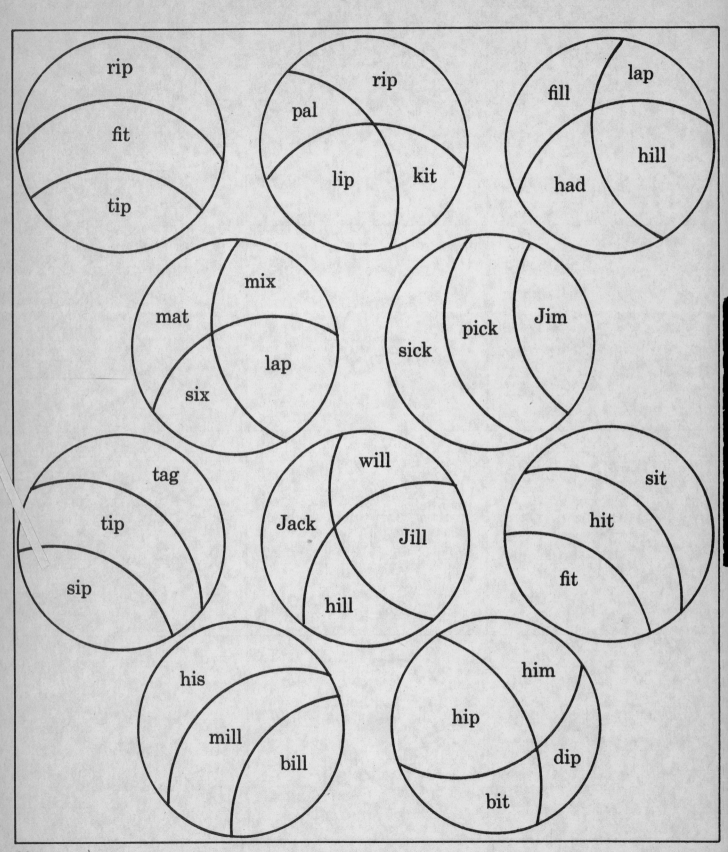

UNIT 2: Short vowel I.
DIRECTIONS: Below each picture, print the name of the picture and a word that rhymes with it. Color all the pictures.

UNIT 2: Short vowel I.
DIRECTIONS: Complete each sentence using all the words in the box.

1. Dick will go _____ .	the to hill
2. Sam has a _____ .	ham big fat
3. Ann and Dick will _____ .	go Bill with
4. The cat will _____ .	the rip sack
5. The lid will fit _____ .	pan big the
6. The man will _____ .	six quit at
7. Bill will _____ .	the bat fix

UNIT 2:   Short vowels A and I.
DIRECTIONS: Read each sentence. Draw a circle around the correct word, and print it on the line.

1. Mother has a blue _____.   like   limp   lamp

2. Dan gave the _____ to Ann.   give   gift   lift

3. I _____ going with Jim.   and   am   an

4. The man _____ not see me.   hid   had   did

5. The children _____ to school.   ran   rain   fan

6. Mother gave me _____.   like   mile   milk

7. The things are in a _____.   big   bag   bat

8. Dad will _____ the lamp.   play   mix   fix

9. We came to school in a _____.   came   cap   cab

10. The boys played in the _____.   kind   hand   sand

11. The _____ came to see Dad.   man   mat   make

12. Little _____ have lots of fun.   pigs   pins   figs

13. Jim _____ in the cab.   sing   fat   sat

14. Baby is on Mother's _____.   limp   lap   lip

15. Dick _____ go on the bus.   with   will   wag

16. We _____ fun at school.   hit   hid   had

UNIT 2: Short vowel U.
DIRECTIONS: Draw a circle around the name of the picture. In the box, print the vowel that
you hear in the word.

cap cup	gas gun	Dick duck
kit	gum	Dad
can cup	jug jig	tug tip
cap	just	bug
but nuts	calf cut	sack six
nap	cuff	sick
sun sum	as bun	ask ax
dim	bus	is

UNIT 2: Short vowel U.
DIRECTIONS: Read the words in the block above the pictures, and find the picture that goes
with each word. Print the name of each picture in the space below it.

bud	cup	rug	bus	bug	sun
gum	pup	gun	tub	jug	duck

UNIT 2: Short vowel U.
DIRECTIONS: Read each riddle. Find the correct answer, and print it on the line.

Boys have fun with me.	I can say, "Bow wow."	You can eat me.
What am I?	What am I?	What am I?
dug gun	cup up	cut but
fun run	pup cut	fun nut
I am little.	I can have milk in me.	We like to do this.
What am I?	What am I?	What is it?
bus tub	up cut	just lump
sun bug	cup cuff	muff jump
This is fun to do.	You can ride in me.	You see me in the sky.
What is it?	What am I?	What am I?
fun run	bud bug	sun but
gun sun	bus us	run sum
I say, "Quack."	We do this to Mother.	We do this for Mother.
What am I?	What is it?	What is it?
suck luck	up jump	just dug
pup duck	sun hug	dust rust

DIRECTIONS: Draw a circle around the word that belongs in the sentence, and print it on the line.

1. Baby saw a yellow_____at the farm.

   dock   luck   duck   tuck

2. Mother gave me a_____ of hot tea.

   pup   bus   cup   bug

3. One day I went to town in a big _____.

   just   bus   dust   must

4. When I play, I like to_____rope.

   jump   mumps   bump   lump

5. At Jack's house we had candy and _____.

   but   cut   hut   nuts

6. Mother has a blue_____for the house.

   tug   lug   rug   dug

7. I like to run and play in the _____.

   gun   sun   gum   dug

UNIT 2: Short vowels A, I, U.
DIRECTIONS: Make new words by changing the vowels. Print the new words on the lines.

Can you help Jack?

Can you help Jill?

	i	u
bat		
bag		
sack		
ham		
bad		
hat		
as		
fan		

UNIT 2: Short vowels A, I, U.
DIRECTIONS: Have fun with these questions. Draw a circle around the correct answer.

1.	Can a black gun run fast?	Yes	No
2.	Is a big cup a little nut?	Yes	No
3.	Is the sun black?	Yes	No
4.	Can a cat run fast?	Yes	No
5.	Can a big pig sing for you?	Yes	No
6.	Is a cube a baby duck?	Yes	No
7.	Can a pup run up a tree?	Yes	No
8.	Is a green rug red?	Yes	No
9.	Is Ann a big man?	Yes	No
10.	Can you go up a hill?	Yes	No
11.	Can a little cup do a funny jig?	Yes	No
12.	Can a cat kill a rat?	Yes	No
13.	Can you fill a pan with milk?	Yes	No
14.	Can a doll run to get milk?	Yes	No
15.	Can a pig go as fast as a cab?	Yes	No
16.	Can you rub your hands?	Yes	No
17.	Is a sad girl happy?	Yes	No
18.	Can a bug cut a bun?	Yes	No
19.	Can a pig dig in the mud?	Yes	No

UNIT 2: Short vowel O.
DIRECTIONS: Read the words in the block above the pictures. Find the picture that goes with
the word, and print the word in the space below it.

top	mop	pot	box	Tom	sock
cot	doll	fox	lock	rock	rod

UNIT 2: Short vowel O.
DIRECTIONS: Read the sentences, and do as they tell you. Then draw a blue line under all the
short O words.

1. Do you see the cot? Draw a circle around the cot. Color the cot red.

2. See the lock? Color it green. Make a black dot near it.

3. Can you see the rock? Color it red. Draw a black line under it.

4. Look at the doll. Color her hat blue. Color her dress yellow.

5. See Bob? Make a little red X under him. Color Bob.

6. Do you see the fox? Color the fox yellow. Draw a box around the fox.

7. See the mop? Color it blue. Make two red dots near the mop.

8. Look at the top. Draw a black X on it. Color it red and blue.

UNIT 2: Short vowel O.
DIRECTIONS: Draw a line under the sentence that tells about the picture. Draw a box around each short O word in the sentences.

	The fox ran to the house.
	The fox is in the box.
	The fox is next to the tree.
	The box is next to the tree.
	Don is playing with a top.
	Bob sat on a big rock.
	Don is on top of the big rock.
	Tom has a big rock in his hand.
	The dog ran to the box.
	The mop is not in the box.
	I will hop, hop, hop to the log.
	See the doll in the box.
	I got the doll from my father.
	Jill can see the top spin.
	The little top is on the cot.
	The little top is in Bob's hand.
	We will not stop here.
	Baby Doll is in the box.
	The milk in the cup is hot.
	The big red top is for Baby.

UNIT 2: Short vowel O.

UNIT 2: Short vowel O.
DIRECTIONS: Draw a circle around the word that tells the name of the picture.

six fix	bun hit	doll bill	tan fan
sit sun	box fox	dot dog	fun fin
cup cap	mat cot	sick sock	rock luck
kit can	mop pop	son suck	lock sock
fix fox	pin top	tick rack	pot dug
box fun	pot tip	tuck rock	dog log

UNIT 2:   Short vowels A, I, U, O.
DIRECTIONS: Print the name of each picture in the space below it.

UNIT 2: Short vowels A, I, U, O.
DIRECTIONS: Read each sentence. Draw a circle around the correct word, and print it on the line.

1. The little _____ can say, "Quack."   sick

2. We can not play if we are_____.   duck

3. Dad will ride in the_____.   Jack

4. Dick and_____will go to school.   bus

5. Bill lost his green_____.   dog

6. A_____can say, "Bow wow."   top

7. The doll fell_____the box.   fi

8. Father will_____the tent.   ff

1. Jim and Dan are_____school.   us

2. Ann_____up the big hill.   rock

3. Dad has a gift for_____.   in

4. Tom sat on the big_____.   ran

5. The nuts are in the_____.   bag

6. Baby gave Mother a_____.   hug

7. Did the_____see the man with the gun?   am

8. I_____going to town with Mother.   fox

35

UNIT 2: Short vowel E.

DIRECTIONS: Print the name of the picture on the line that has the same number as the picture. Color the pictures.

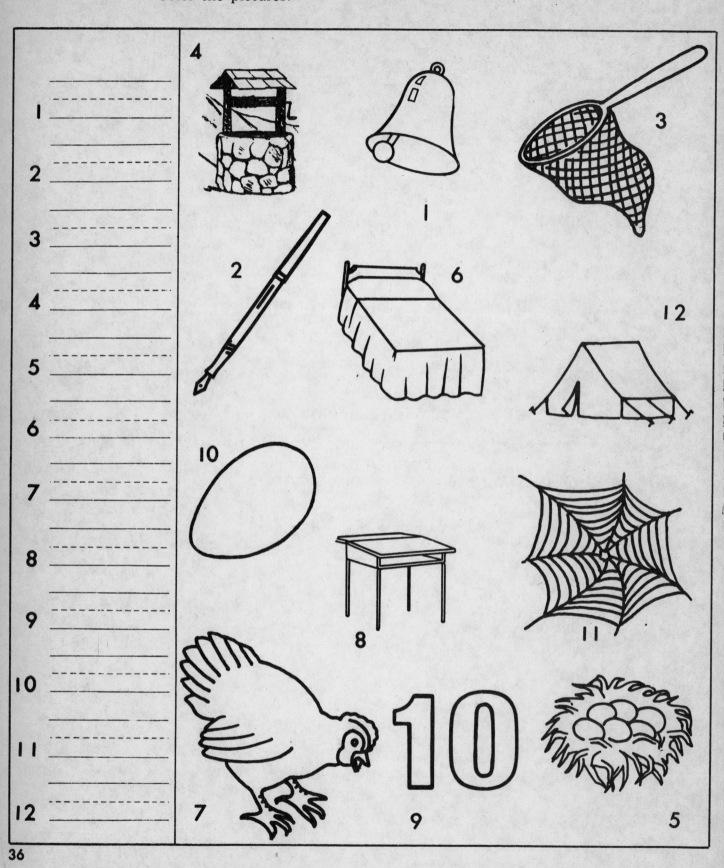

1 _____
2 _____
3 _____
4 _____
5 _____
6 _____
7 _____
8 _____
9 _____
10 _____
11 _____
12 _____

UNIT 2: Short vowel E.
DIRECTIONS: Print the name of the picture. Read each sentence below, and print "yes" or "no" on the line .

1. You sleep in a bed.

2. It is fun to play with a big fox.

3. A bell is the same as a box.

4. We like to run and play.

5. A cat has six legs.

6. A big tree can jump up and down.

7. A lad can help his father.

8. You can go fast in a jet plane.

9. A doll is just the same as a fox.

10. Jim will be a man when he gets big.

11. An ant is as big as an ox.

UNIT 2: Short vowels A, I, U, O, E.
DIRECTIONS: Read each sentence. Change the vowel in the word that comes after the sentence to make a new word that will fit in the sentence. Print it on the line.

Ann is in _____ .   bud

Jim has milk in the _____ .   cap

Mother will _____ eggs.   got

Don is _____ in bed.   sack

Th___ _____ can see the rat.   cot

Tom will go with _____ .   did

The children like to _____ .   hip

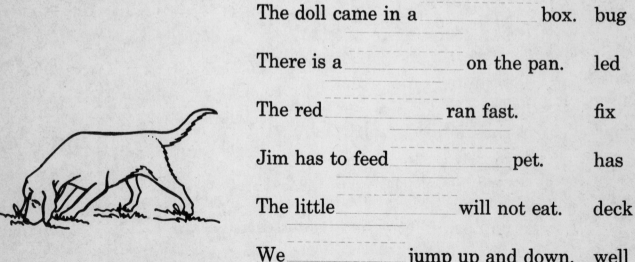

Jim will play with his _____ .   dig

The doll came in a _____ box.   bug

There is a _____ on the pan.   led

The red _____ ran fast.   fix

Jim has to feed _____ pet.   has

The little _____ will not eat.   deck

We _____ jump up and down.   well

40

UNIT 2:   TEST: Short vowels.
DIRECTIONS: In the first part of the test, print the name of each picture. In the second part,
change the vowel to make a new word. In the third part, find the missing word.

Print the name of the picture.

_____   _____   _____   _____

Change the vowel to make a new word.

rod   _____   hit   _____   sick   _____

met   _____   ten   _____   fun   _____

is   _____   cap   _____   bed   _____

but   _____   lamp   _____   pot   _____

Find the missing word.

1.   A dog can _____.   4.   The milk is in the _____.

2.   Baby is in _____.   5.   The box is _____.

3.   Tom will spin the _____.   6.   Jill had on a yellow _____.

bed   cup   run   big   top   hat

41

UNIT 2: Short vowels in compound words and two-syllable words.
DIRECTIONS: In the first part, make two words out of each word you see. In the second part, the name of each picture has two syllables; see if you can print the missing syllable in the space.

Make two words out of each word.

tenpins			upon	
catfish			cannot	
tiptop			bathtub	
himself			sunset	
gumdrops			uphill	
milkman			windmill	

Print the missing part.

k i t _____

rab _____

mit _____

_____ ket

_____ py

_____ kin

UNIT 3:   Long vowel A.
DIRECTIONS: Read each sentence. Find the missing word, and print it on the line.

If a one-part word (or syllable) has two vowels, the first vowel is usually long and the second one is silent.

cane   pail   rake

1. What is the big boy's_____?   late

2. We must not be_____for school.   rain

3. Father has green_____in the can.   cane

4. The_____fell on the house.   paint

5. The lame man must use a_____.   made

6. Mother _____ a cake for John.   name

1. Mother will_____milk to the baby.   paid

2. Jim_____the man for the milk.   lake

3. It is fun to sail a boat on the_____.   vase

4. Father just_____home from work.   take

5. The dog likes to sit near the_____.   gate

6. Tom gave a red_____to Mother.   came

DIRECTIONS: Read the riddles and the answers. Draw a circle around the correct answer.

can

I am made of tin.

I am not good to eat.

What am I?

cane   cap   cake   can

cane

You can play in me.

You can sail a boat on me.

What am I?

wake   lap   lake   back

Jack and Jill had me.

They put something in me.

What am I?

pal   tail   pail   pat

You can eat me.

I help make you big.

What am I?

rat   tame   same   ham

I am good to eat.

Mother can bake me.

What am I?

cape   cake   cap   cat

I can be your pet.

I do not like dogs.

What am I?

cap   cape   cat   Kate

I am a girl.

I have a little name.

Who am I?

Dan   Dad   Am   Jane

UNIT 3: Long vowel I.
DIRECTIONS: In the first part, print the name of the picture in the space under it; the words in the middle of the page will help you. In the second part, draw a line under the long I words. In the third part, find the long I word and print it on the line.

Draw a line under the long I words.

dime	pipe	pin	five	ripe	sit	tie
bite	nine	mile	ride	hide	kite	fire

Find the long I word and print it in the space.

1. Mother gave us _____ cakes.   fix   five   fire

2. The little boy played with his _____.   kite   kit   hide

3. I will _____ down the hill on my sled.   hide   rid   ride

4. My dad gave me a blue _____.   bake   hike   bike

5. I gave Dad a _____.   ripe   pipe   rip

6. We must not play with _____.   fire   fin   five

UNIT 3: Long vowel I.
DIRECTIONS: In the first part, draw a box around the name of the picture. In the second part, read the sentence and print the correct answer on the line.

Draw a box around the name of the picture.

| fin | fire | pig | pile | bike | big | bib | bite |

Print the answer on the line.

I will pay a _____ for it.

| dime | dim | dill |

Bill will _____ the ball.

| hat | hill | hit |

He will ride his _____ .

| big | bike | like |

Jack made a big _____ .

| fit | fine | fire |

A bug has _____ legs.

| sick | silly | six |

We saw the goats and the _____ .

| piles | pigs | bibs |

She will bake a _____ .

| pipe | pie | pill |

She was _____ .

| tick | bill | sick |

46

DIRECTIONS: Choose the correct word, and print it on the line.

1. We did it when we played.	_____	rain	ran	man
2. We did it to Mother's cake.	_____	at	late	ate
3. A dog has it.	_____	tail	pail	pat
4. We can do it to a coat.	_____	rip	pipe	ripe
5. It likes to eat.	_____	pit	pin	pig
6. Mother can do it.	_____	bake	back	lake
7. We can do it in a bus.	_____	rid	ride	like
8. A can has this.	_____	did	died	lid
9. It is the name of a girl.	_____	Cat	Jane	Bat
10. It is the name of a tree.	_____	pin	time	pine
11. We do this to dishes.	_____	whip	wipe	wide
12. It is the name of a boy.	_____	Jill	Jane	Jack
13. We like to eat it.	_____	bit	pie	pat
14. We can ride it.	_____	bill	bat	bike
15. A boy can put it on.	_____	tip	tie	time
16. A dog can do this.	_____	bit	pit	bite
17. It falls from the sky.	_____	ran	rip	rain

UNIT 3: Long vowel U.
DIRECTIONS: Read each sentence. Draw a circle around the correct answer. Then find the long U word in each sentence. Print it on the line below.

1.	A red vase is blue.	Yes	No
2.	A mule can kick.	Yes	No
3.	I can use soap to clean my hands.	Yes	No
4.	A cube can play with a bat.	Yes	No
5.	A mule has two tails.	Yes	No
6.	Baby ducks are cute.	Yes	No
7.	We play in the sun in June.	Yes	No
8.	An ice cube is cold.	Yes	No
9.	You can eat a suit.	Yes	No
10.	A tube is a top that can sing.	Yes	No
11.	We use desks in school.	Yes	No
12.	We can sing a little tune.	Yes	No

1. _____

2. _____

3. _____

4. _____

5. _____

6. _____

7. _____

8. _____

9. _____

10. _____

11. _____

12. _____

UNIT 3: Long vowel U.
DIRECTIONS: Print the long U words on the long U ladder. Print the short U words on the short U ladder.

suit

must

cake

just

duck

fire

jump

cute

tune

bump

tube

dug

cube

mule

nut

fuse

pipe

use

bud

Long U

Short U

UNIT 3: Long vowels A, I, U.

DIRECTIONS: Read the words below. If the word is a long vowel word, print L on the line.
If the word is a short vowel word, print S on the line.

late	_____	June	_____	mule	_____
man	_____	milk	_____	rake	_____
rain	_____	pick	_____	six	_____
use	_____	cute	_____	cap	_____
bat	_____	time	_____	fun	_____
suit	_____	lick	_____	us	_____
map	_____	wide	_____	gate	_____
tame	_____	pie	_____	tune	_____
lap	_____	ate	_____	ride	_____
up	_____	pill	_____	make	_____
tube	_____	cut	_____	fill	_____
bake	_____	wipe	_____	nut	_____

DIRECTIONS: Read each sentence. Draw a circle around the correct word, and print it on the line.

1. I paid a _____ for the candy.   dim   dime   cat

2. Do not _____ from me.   died   hide   hid

3. Dan will _____ his boat.   sail   pal   tail

4. Sue has _____ blue cups.   fix   fan   six

5. Mother gave Jim a red _____ .   sun   tie   sit

6. My pet is called _____ .   Tim   Time   Take

7. A boy takes off his _____ at home.   nap   cap   kit

8. Jack can play with _____ .   Tune   Tim   Time

9. Baby _____ milk to drink.   had   hid   use

10. Mother will _____ a white cake.   back   bake   bike

11. The _____ came down fast.   fine   ran   rain

12. She ate a little _____ .   cake   tug   bake

13. The little _____ likes to play.   cape   cat   fat

14. Mother will _____ us to the party.   like   tack   take

15. The _____ is still hot.   pin   pie   tie

16. Mother has the _____ for the box.   lad   lid   laid

UNIT 3: Long vowel O.

DIRECTIONS: Print L in front of the long O words at the top of the page. Read each of the sentences, find the missing word and print it on the line.

Print L in front of the long O words.

_____ coat	_____ got	_____ Joan	_____ boat	_____ rope
_____ rod	_____ road	_____ coke	_____ pot	_____ rode

Print the missing word on the line.

1. The big girl's name is_____.   boat

2. The dog will hide his_____.   road

3. See the big_____on the lake.   hole

4. The girl had on a red_____.   bone

5. I will run_____to Mother.   home

6. The dog dug a_____for his bone.   Joan

7. We_____the bus to school.   joke

8. Jim sent a_____ to Mother.   hope

9. The girls like to jump_____.   rode

10. Father played a_____on us.   coat

11. The cab ran off the_____and into the lake.   note

12. I_____it will not rain.   rope

DIRECTIONS: Print the name of each picture in the space below it. Read each sentence, find
a word that will complete the sentence and also rhyme with the word that
follows the sentence. Print the correct answer on the line.

Print the names of the pictures.

_____

_____

_____

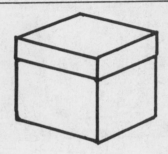

_____

_____

_____

Find the missing word.

1. I _____ it will not rain this week.   rope

2. Dick can not find his little blue _____.   cop

3. Mother has a vase for the _____.   nose

4. The big _____ likes to eat hens.   box

5. Jim has a little pet _____.   fog

6. Ann is eating a big _____.   zone

DIRECTIONS: Draw a circle around the name of the picture. Read the sentences, find the correct answer, and print it on the line.

Draw a circle around the name of the picture.

hat   hate | kit   kite | got   goat

cot   coat | pal   pail | tub   tube

Find the missing word.

1.   Jane can jump_____.   suit

2.   The boys sat on a rock by the_____.   bat

3.   Jim rode home from school on his_____.   cake

4.   Ann wants to bake a_____.   bike

5.   Jack hit the ball with his_____.   rope

6.   James put on his blue _____.   cot

7.   The man went to sleep on the_____.   cut

8.   Let Jane_____the birthday cake.   lake

UNIT 3: Long vowels A, I, U, O.
DIRECTIONS: Draw a line under the word that fits the sentence, and print it on the line.

1. I＿＿＿＿＿that you will come.   hop   hope

2. The lame man has to use a＿＿＿＿.   can   cane

3. Baby Sue is a＿＿＿＿little girl.   cut   cute

4. Did Mother＿＿＿＿the ham?   cut   cute

5. Did you＿＿＿＿the baby's blocks?   hid   hide

6. Mother will take＿＿＿＿to town.   us   use

7. I lost a＿＿＿＿on the way home.   dime   dim

8. Did you＿＿＿＿the game?   wine   win

9. The little pig＿＿＿＿five pies.   at   ate

10. Please＿＿＿＿the rose on my coat.   pine   pin

11. You may＿＿＿＿my pen.   use   us

12. I will fly in a＿＿＿＿.   plan   plane

13. I＿＿＿＿that you will win.   hop   hope

14. Jim is near the＿＿＿＿tree.   pin   pine

15. Miss Dell sent a＿＿＿＿to Mother.   not   note

16. Jack had a big＿＿＿＿of pie.   bite   bit

17. He＿＿＿＿the last cupcake.   at   ate

UNIT 3: Long vowel E.
DIRECTIONS: Read each sentence. Draw a circle around the long E word in each sentence, and print it on the line.

1. The pipe has a leak.

2. A yellow leaf fell on the desk.

3. Mother made tea for lunch.

4. Ann has ten yellow beads.

5. I can see Don's tent.

6. Ted ate a big meal.

7. The bug bit Jean on the leg.

8. Bill rode in Ned's jeep.

9. I will keep this fish for Ben.

10. The big doll is for Baby Jean.

11. Do you feel well?

12. Mother had red beets for lunch.

13. Will you heat the milk for Baby?

14. The well is deep.

15. The meat is in the pan.

16. Dad had a fine seat at the game.

17. I like to read for you.

UNIT 3: Long vowel E.
DIRECTIONS: Read each sentence. Draw a circle around the correct word, and print it on the line.

1. Jane came to school and sat in her _____.

          get   seen   seat

2. Mother will need three _____ for the cake.

          end   peg   eggs

3. Spot cut his _____ on the rocks.

          beat   feet   beet

4. Ann is going to _____.

          bed   bead   leg

5. Jim's dog can sit up and beg for _____.

          mean   met   meat

6. Jean and Jack _____ Mr. Hill.

          set   let   met

7. The eggs are in the _____.

          best   nest   beast

8. The boy has the fish in the _____.

          neat   net   get

9. It was late when Jane went to _____.

          bed   let   bet

10. We will take a trip next _____.

          weed   feet   week

DIRECTIONS: In the first part, find a picture whose name contains the sound asked for, and print the number of the picture on the line. In the second part, print on the lines two words that rhyme with the given word.

4

5

6

7

3

Find the picture.

Short a	____	Long e	____
Short i	____	Long a	____
Short u	____	Long o	____
Short e	____	Long u	____
Short o	____	Long i	____

8

Print two rhyming words.

hat ____ ____

went ____ ____

gate ____ ____

like ____ ____

fun ____ ____

seed ____ ____

2

1

9

10

UNIT 3: Long and short vowels and rhyming.

DIRECTIONS: In the first part, change the first vowel in each word to form a new word and print it on the line. In the second part, find a word in column 2 that rhymes with a word in column 1 and print it on the line.

Print the new word.

cop _____	wide _____	Jean _____	had _____
like _____	Tom _____	but _____	bake _____
hop _____	bug _____	rode _____	ride _____

Find the rhyming word.

1		**2**	**1**		**2**
time	_____	tube	seat	_____	tin
mat	_____	cub	us	_____	heat
cube	_____	cape	fin	_____	tub
big	_____	dime	cub	_____	cob
ten	_____	box	hope	_____	bus
rub	_____	feed	bet	_____	rope
need	_____	dig	rob	_____	ride
tape	_____	fat	ate	_____	late
fox	_____	men	hide	_____	get

UNIT 3: Long and short vowels.
DIRECTIONS: Say the name of the picture. Color the S box if the vowel is short; the L box if it is long. In the last box, print the vowel you hear.

UNIT 3: TEST: Long and short vowels.
DIRECTIONS: Read each sentence. Draw a circle around the correct word, and print it on the line.

1. I have a _____ for candy.　　　　dim　　dime　　time

2. My name is _____ .　　　　　　　Tom　　Time　　Tube

3. The boy sat in the _____ .　　　　tub　　rub　　cub

4. This cub will not _____ you.　　　bit　　bite　　kite

5. Jane's doll is _____ .　　　　　　rut　　cube　　cute

6. Dick will _____ the ball.　　　　bat　　cat　　pill

7. Father has the eggs in a _____ .　fox　　sail　　box

8. Did you drop the _____ ?　　　　cut　　cute　　cup

9. Ann has _____ dolls.　　　　　　see　　three　　tree

10. Tom will sail his _____ .　　　　cot　　boat　　coat

11. The boy has a red _____ .　　　coat　　bit　　tell

12. The girl sleeps on the _____ .　　cot　　say　　not

13. A _____ was in the cave.　　　　cube　　made　　cub

14. The _____ ran on the tracks.　　train　　pail　　mail

15. The dog ate the _____ .　　　　met　　meat　　seat

16. The boy _____ by the tree.　　　hid　　hide　　had

17. The man _____ down the street.　went　　want　　sent

61

UNIT 3: Long vowels in compound words.

DIRECTIONS: In each box, take a word from the first column and combine it with a word from the second column to form a new word. Then use the words in the sentences below.

Make new words.

rain	_____	meal	bee	_____	stack
sail	_____	coat	air	_____	mate
oat	_____	man	fire	_____	plane
drive	_____	boat	play	_____	hive
mail	_____	way	hay	_____	men

Find the missing words.

1. The _____ gave me a letter.

2. The big truck went up the _____.

3. My _____ keeps me dry.

4. Did you see the _____ on the lake?

5. Mother gave us _____ to eat.

6. The _____ rode on the big red truck.

7. The bees flew into the _____.

8. The hen hid in the _____.

9. His father gave him a ride in an _____.

10. My _____ has a boat, too.

62

UNIT 3: Compound and two-syllable words.
DIRECTIONS: Choose two words to make a new word, and print it on the line. At the bottom of the page, combine a syllable in the first column with one in the second column to form a word. Print the word on the line.

pea	hand	weed
sea	bag	nut

_____
- - - - - - - - - - - - - - - - -
_____
_____
- - - - - - - - - - - - - - - - -
_____

meal	up	set
my	oat	self

_____
- - - - - - - - - - - - - - - - -
_____
_____
- - - - - - - - - - - - - - - - -
_____

tree	rain	man
coat	fire	top

_____
- - - - - - - - - - - - - - - - -
_____
_____
- - - - - - - - - - - - - - - - -
_____

stack	mate	rail
road	hay	play

_____
- - - - - - - - - - - - - - - - -
_____
_____
- - - - - - - - - - - - - - - - -
_____

Make words.

bun	pen	_____
hap	ny	_____
tick	kin	_____
nap	et	_____

tab	ner	_____
kit	ny	_____
din	let	_____
pen	ten	_____

63

DIRECTIONS: Use the words at the top of the page to complete the sentences. At the bottom of the page, divide each word in the list into two words.

Find the missing words.

flagpole	raindrops	hillside	haystack	fireman
bedtime	raincoat	pancakes	cannot	inside

1. You will need your _____.

2. We had _____ for dinner.

3. The man came to paint the _____.

4. Mother likes to hear the _____.

5. It is _____ for Baby Ann.

6. A _____ must be brave.

7. The sheep ate grass on the _____.

8. We had fun jumping up and down in the _____.

9. It rained, so the children had to go _____.

10. Sue _____ go with you to the farm.

Draw a box around the two little words in each big word.

seaweed	himself	skyline	airplane
wayside	firefly	sunshine	playtime
teapot	into	itself	railroad
milkman	mailman	treetop	birdhouse

UNIT 3: Auditory recognition of hard and soft C.

DIRECTIONS: Say the name of each picture. Color the picture orange if its name contains the sound of soft C. Color it blue if its name contains the sound of hard C.

When C is followed by E, I, or Y, the C is usually soft.

fence	cap	clock
cup	pencil	cake
mice	candle	camel
coat	face	car

DIRECTIONS: Read the sentence. Find the correct word, and print it on the line.

Find the missing words.

1. The children will run in the _____ .
   mice   race   nice   next

2. Father put a cube of _____ in the cup.
   pink   city   face   ice

3. The three gray _____ ran to the barn.
   pay   mice   nice   nuts

4. John went to buy some _____ .
   coat   city   face   candy

5. Joan's yellow dress had _____ on it.
   lazy   lace   face   lunch

6. You must find a mask for your _____ .
   face   fast   fame   fact

7. Ten _____ is the same as a dime.
   sense   sent   cents   since

8. Our class will go to the _____ .
   circus   since   send   sent

9. The _____ was filled with people.
   coat   city   cents   lace

10. We can print with a _____ .
    pencil   celery   cigar   camel

UNIT 3: Hard and soft G.
DIRECTIONS: The letter G has two sounds—hard and soft. Print the words at the top of the page on the correct lines.

When G is followed by E, I, or Y, the G is usually soft.

gem	goes	gym	goat	age
gin	Gene	flag	game	gas
stage	egg	gave	gun	page
good	dog	cage	giant	change

Soft g words

Hard g words

UNIT 3:   Hard and soft C and G.
DIRECTIONS: Draw a blue line under the words in the list that have the hard sound of C or G.
Print in the bubbles the words that have the soft sound of C and G.

price

mice

grand

age

stage

games

change

cent

gem

ice

gym

cake

cell

gin

race

rice

gas

candy

trace

giant

UNIT 3: TEST: Hard and soft C and G.
DIRECTIONS: Print S if the word has a soft C or G; print H if the word has a hard sound of
C or G. At the bottom of the page, draw a red box around the soft G words,
and a blue box around the soft C words.

Print S or H.

place _____ cuff _____ ice _____ carry _____ gin _____ cash _____

grand _____ trace _____ candy _____ age _____ came _____ coast _____

catch _____ class _____ Nancy _____ gym _____ cent _____ gypsy _____

flag _____ space _____ care _____ goes _____ cage _____ Cindy _____

page _____ mice _____ rice _____ gem _____ ugly _____ care _____

lace _____ slice _____ camp _____ flag _____ Gene _____ brace _____

Draw a blue box around the soft c words.
Draw a red box around the soft g words.

1. Grace gave Jim a cage.

2. Will you bake ginger cakes?

3. The strange prince danced on the stage.

4. The gray mice ate a box of rice.

5. Fudge candy costs ten cents.

6. George saw a strange man on the large bridge.

7. Some mice were eating candy by the fence.

8. The gypsy camp is close to the city.

DIRECTIONS: Look at each picture. Print the correct blend in the space. At the bottom of the page, print the word that answers the riddle.

A blend is two or three consonants sounded together.

____ apes   ____ og   ____ um   ____ ee

____ o s s

You can eat me.

I can be green or blue.

I am on a vine.

I am a _____.

____ u i t

I am green.	I am at the store.
I am in your yard.	I am good to eat.
Birds stay in me.	I help make you big.
I am a _____.	I am _____.
I am red and yellow.	I can jump and hop.
Boys play with me.	You find me in a pond.
They like to beat me.	I eat bugs.
I am a _____.	I am a _____.

UNIT 4:   R blends.
DIRECTIONS: Draw a circle around the word that tells the name of the picture. Find the blends
in the words in the list at the bottom of the page, and print them on the line.

Draw a circle around the name of the picture.

grapes	trim	trade	drive
grass	truck	tree	drum
grade	train	trap	drink

from	train	drapes	grapes
fruit	truck	dress	grass
frost	trick	drum	grade

Print the blends.

bring _____	grass _____	drum _____
fry _____	brave _____	cross _____
trip _____	trick _____	brick _____
grape _____	grain _____	fruit _____
grade _____	bride _____	trade _____
train _____	grab _____	free _____

71

UNIT 4: L blends.
DIRECTIONS: On the line near the picture, print the L blend that you hear. Then read the sentences
at the bottom of the page, draw a circle around the correct answer, and print it
on the line.

Print the L blends you hear.

Find the missing word.

1. Jim will play with his red_____.   slip   sled

2. Mother broke the blue_____.   please   plate

3. The milk is in the_____.   glass   class

4. See the big_____wave.   flat   flag

5. Jean gave Tom a_____.   play   plum

6. Ted's dog is_____and white.   block   black

7. This_____will win the prize.   clap   class

8. The_____are in the vases.   plants   play

UNIT 4: L blends.
DIRECTIONS: Read each riddle, and print the answer in the space. The picture will help you.
Then read each sentence, choose the correct word from the list and print it on
the line.

Answer the riddles.

I tick-tock the time.

Sometimes I chime.

What am I?

_____

High up on a pole

I flap and I blow.

What am I?

_____

Find the missing words.

1. Mother set the cake on a _____ .   plane

2. Baby made a house with his _____ .   float

3. The _____ is made of silk.   clock

4. The red _____ went up, up, up.   flag

5. A _____ tells us the time.   clap

6. My boat can _____ on the lake.   blocks

7. Baby likes to _____ her hands.   glass

8. The milk is in the _____ .   plate

9. Tom will ride his red _____ .   bleed

10. Did the cut on his hand _____ ?   sled

UNIT 4:   R and L blends.
DIRECTIONS: Say the name of each picture, and print in the box the blend that you hear at the beginning of its name.

UNIT 4:   R and L blends.
DIRECTIONS: Print the name of the pictures in the spaces below the pictures. Draw a circle around the correct word below each sentence, and print it on the line.

Print the names of the pictures.

Find the missing words.

1.   Did you see the _____ fly over the pond?

   from   crow   frost

2.   My dog is _____ and white.

   blade   bless   black

3.   Father came home and cut the _____.

   grass   grab   grape

4.   The fish is on the _____.

   plate   play   plum

5.   Tom can beat his _____.

   drum   dress   drink

6.   An oak _____ is near Jack's house.

   trick   tree   trip

UNIT 4: S blends.

DIRECTIONS: Say the name of the picture in each box. Think of the consonant blend with which it begins. Print the blend in the box. The list of blends will help you.

sc	st	sp	sn	squ
scr	str	sl	sm	sw

UNIT 4: S blends.
DIRECTIONS: Read the sentence. Find the correct word in the list, and print it on the line. Then draw a circle around the word below each picture that tells the name of the picture.

Find the missing words.

1. Do not _____ the milk.   skate

2. Did you _____ to Father?   speak

3. Green means go and red means _____.   snake

4. Can you _____ on ice?   smoke

5. Jim saw a _____ near the barn.   smell

6. I can _____ those nice flowers.   stop

7. Grandfather likes to _____ a pipe.   stripes

8. The flag has red and white _____.   spill

Draw a circle around the names of the pictures.

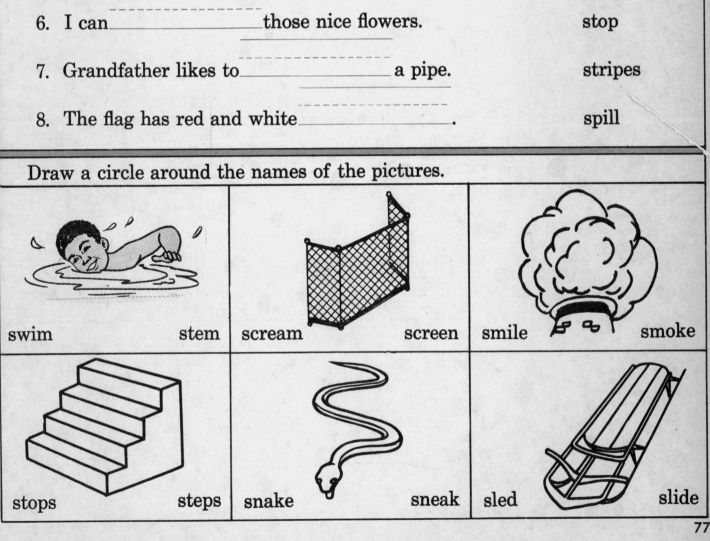

| swim | stem | scream | screen | smile | smoke |

| stops | steps | snake | sneak | sled | slide |

77

UNIT 4:   Review of blends.

DIRECTIONS: Say the name of the picture. Think of the consonant blend with which its name begins, and print the blend on the line.

UNIT 4:   Review of blends.

DIRECTIONS: Read the sentence. Draw a circle around the consonant blend that will complete the sentence. Print it on the line.

1. The cake is on the_____ate.   br   pl   sm

2. Did you win the_____ize?   cl   sn   pr

3. Bob_____ove the blue car.   dr   gl   sc

4. The_____ack cat ran away.   squ   gr   bl

5. Can you see the_____ane?   pl   sk   br

6. I will_____ay home.   cr   fl   st

7. Do you like to eat_____ums?   pl   ___   scr

8. Jim_____oke his drum.   sp   bl   b

9. I like to see the_____ag wave.   tr   st   fl

10. Will you_____ink the milk?   dr   sl   bl

11. I saw a_____ane in the sky.   scr   pl   gl

12. The hill is white with _____ ow.   dr   sn   cr

13. Did you see the big _____ake?   fr   sn   gl

14. Mother likes her _____ants.   pl   dr   squ

15. See me ride my red _____ed.   gr   sl   sm

16. The fish _____im in the pond.   sw   gr   bl

UNIT 4: Review of blends.
DIRECTIONS: Read each sentence. Change the blend in the word at the right to make a new word that will complete the sentence. Print the new word on the line.

1. Father is going to cut the _____ .   glass

2. We must cut the meat on the _____ .   skate

3. Do not play in the _____ .   greet

4. Dave likes to play his red _____ .   plum

5. The robins made a nest in the _____ .   free

6. It is fun to _____ in the lake.   trim

7. I will help Mother _____ the steps.   sleep

8. The man did some funny _____ .   bricks

9. Do not _____ the boat from the baby.   crab

10. Jim likes to play _____ on us.   sticks

11. Don made a house with his _____ .   flocks

12. I had a _____ of milk for dinner.   brass

13. We had fun on the _____ .   bring

14. I can _____ the red roses.   spell

15. Dick can _____ his top.   skin

16. Last week I had a funny _____ .   scream

80

UNIT 4: TEST: Consonant blends.
DIRECTIONS: In the exercise at the top, choose the correct blend to complete the sentence and print it on the line. In the exercise at the bottom, use the blend in the column at the right to make a word to complete the sentence. Print the word on the line.

Find the missing blends.

1. Joan's _____ue dress was in the box.   bl   fl   str

2. We _____ile when we are happy.   sn   sm   sp

3. Jim _____oke the glass plate.   sl   sk   br

4. When we ask for something we say _____ease.   sp   pr   pl

5. Last week we played with the _____eds.   sw   sl   gl

6. The cat went up the _____ee.   tr   fr   str

7. Joe likes to _____im in the lake.   cr   sc   sw

Print the missing words.

1. The little _____ sat near the pond.   fr

2. We drink milk from a _____.   gl

3. Father will cut the _____.   gr

4. The men painted the _____ pole.   fl

5. Do not leave your _____ on the steps.   sk

6. My house is on this _____.   str

7. The baby is in the _____.   cr

UNIT 4: Y used as a vowel.
DIRECTIONS: Draw a line under the words in which Y has a sound almost like long E.

baby	cry	why	happy
try	lady	candy	tiny
Patty	sandy	shy	puppy
penny	Jimmy	funny	Billy
try	buggy	dry	my
sleepy	sunny	fly	Betty

1. Jane went to get a box of candy.

2. The puppy bumped into the tray.

3. Pat will play with Baby.

4. Did you see the funny man cry?

5. Tom will get a bunny for his birthday.

6. Betty will help Mother fry the fish.

7. My little puppy is in the box.

8. Bob lost a penny and a dime.

9. Mary will dry the dishes for Mother.

10. Jean is a happy girl.

UNIT 3:   Y used as a vowel.
DIRECTIONS: Draw a line under each word in which Y has a sound almost like long I.

try	Teddy	sly	why	my
fly	dry	candy	rocky	funny
by	windy	taffy	sky	sunny
fry	bunny	happy	Sally	cry
needy	lucky	shy	puppy	Billy

1. Did you see the sly fox?

2. I will try to win the prize.

3. Can you hear the puppy cry?

4. Betty helps Mother dry the dishes.

5. Mother will fry eggs for lunch.

6. The puppy will try to run.

7. Jean is shy in school.

8. Have you seen my little red top?

9. See the plane up in the sky.

10. I set the shell by the box.

UNIT 3: Y used as a vowel.

DIRECTIONS: Choose a Y-word at the bottom of the page to complete each sentence. Then color the balls green that contain words in which Y sounds like long I; color the balls orange that contain words in which Y sounds like long E.

Find the missing word.

1. Mother gave the children_____.

2. _____are you crying?

3. The name of the boy is_____.

4. I will_____the dishes for Mother.

5. Jack's_____dug a hole.

6. The sun is in the_____.

7. Molly will_____to win.

8. The dog did a_____trick.

Teddy   dry   funny   candy   sky

happy   fly   Why

jolly   by   puppy   try

UNIT 3:   TEST: Y used as a vowel.
DIRECTIONS: Look at the picture in each box. Read the words, and draw a circle around each
word that has the same sound of Y as the name of the picture.

Picture	Words	Picture	Words
bunny	baby my fly fifty funny	fairy	sky sunny pony cry Bobby
fly	by try sly poky dry	puppy	lady penny shy fry happy
lily	why silly baby candy bunny	cry	my fairy fly Sally sky
sky	jelly Sandy my fry cry	candy	lucky Billy fifty sky puppy

UNIT 5: AR.
DIRECTIONS: Read the sentence. Find a word in the column at the right that will complete the
sentence, and print it on the line.

barn	star	car

1. We went for a ride in Dad's_____.   park

2. The children played in the_____.   jar

3. The farmer led the sheep into the_____.   star

4. Is the store_____away from here?   car

5. Can you play when it is_____?   arm

6. We went to see Grandfather on the_____.   barn

7. The jam is in the_____.   far

8. Mother looked at my sore_____.   dark

9. Jane will get a_____ for Mother.   card

10. I saw a shiny_____in the sky.   bark

11. Did you hear the dog_____?   farm

12. The kitten played with the_____.   yard

13. Father is out in the back_____.   yarn

UNIT 5: AR.
DIRECTIONS: Look at the word following each sentence. Change the last letter to make a new
word that will complete the sentence. Print the new word on the line. At the
bottom of the page, print two rhyming words under each of the given words.

Make new words.

1.   Fred will mail Dad a _____ .   cart

2.   His little dog likes to _____ .   barn

3.   Baby likes to play in the back _____ .   yarn

4.   I will eat _____ of the pie.   park

5.   Do not try to read in the _____ .   dart

6.   Can you see the _____ in the sky?   start

7.   We made funny cards in _____ class.   arm

8.   We can see goats and pigs in the _____ .   bark

9.   Joe went to play in the _____ .   part

10.   Mother needs more red _____ .   yard

11.   His father can play a _____ .   harm

12.   To begin means to _____ .   stars

Print two rhyming words under each of the words.

mark   start   hard

_____   _____   _____

_____   _____   _____

87

UNIT 5: OR.
DIRECTIONS: Answer the riddle by finding a word that rhymes with the word following the riddle. Print the word on the line.

Jim is thinking of more words.

Will you help him?

1. Something to eat.   horn   _____

2. Something on an ox.   thorn   _____

3. Somthing we eat with.   cork   _____

4. Something to play with.   corn   _____

5. Something on a house.   torch   _____

6. Something that is meat.   fork   _____

7. Something that floats in water.   pork   _____

8. Something that is not long.   port   _____

9. Something on a rose.   born   _____

DIRECTIONS: Find the correct word, and draw a circle around it. Color the pictures.

Jane jar jay	yard yarn yell	barn bark book
home horse horn	clap candy cork	cord card care
car card cost	come corn cart	store stand star
home horse horn	arm are am	form farm fork

UNIT 5: IR, ER, UR.

DIRECTIONS: Underline the words in each column that have the same sound as the picture. At the bottom of the page, print the name of each picture on the line below it.

Find the same sounds.

i r		u r		e r	
	bird		nurse		fern
	fork		purse		sister
	skirt		card		letter
	shirt		church		hammer
	girl		fur		ruler

Print the names of the pictures.

90

UNIT 5: IR, ER, UR.
DIRECTIONS: Underline the word that tells the name of the picture, and color the box that has the same vowel followed by R as the word. At the bottom of the page, find the missing word.

Draw a line under the name of the picture.

	bird			first			tar
	barn			ruler			turkey
	burn			farm			third

| er | or | ir | ir | er | ar | ur | ar | or |

	hammer			shirt			goat
	farmer			skirt			garden
	summer			scarf			girl

| ir | or | er | ar | ir | ur | ir | or | ur |

Find the missing words.

1. The big white rabbit has white_____.
       far   fur   first

2. We can hear the birds_____.
       church   chirp   cheat

3. Tim sent me a_____for my birthday.
       curl   cord   card

4. Ann looked and looked for her_____.
       park   purple   purse

UNIT 5: Review of AR, OR, IR, ER, UR.

DIRECTIONS: In each word find a vowel followed by the letter R. Print the two letters in the first column. In the second column print the number of the picture which has the same two letters in its name.

1. car   2. horn   3. ruler   4. bird   5. nurse

part			forty		
short			storm		
harm			her		
verse			fir		
yard			burn		
turn			port		
perch			park		
pork			horse		
chirp			fur		
jerk			skirt		
first			purse		
party			star		
third			fork		

DIRECTIONS: Draw a line under the letters that will complete the word in each sentence. Print the letters on the line. Answer the riddles at the bottom of the page.

Find the missing letters.

1. The black cat is in the b _____ n.   ar   or   ur

2. Mother has a gray f _____ coat.   or   ur   ar

3. Dan fell and h _____ t his arm.   ur   ar   or

4. See the little f _____ tree.   ar   or   ir

5. We saw red roses in the p _____ k.   er   ar   or

6. Jean sits in the f _____ st seat.   or   ir   ar

7. The c _____ k is in the jug.   ar   er   or

8. Ann swept the d _____ t away.   ir   or   ar

9. The cl _____ k gave me a dime.   ar   er   or

Use these words to answer the riddles below.

bark	dark	corn
skirt	fur	born
park	clerk	car

It is part of a dress.	You like to eat it.	Dogs do this.
A rabbit has it.	You can ride in it.	We play games in it.

93

UNIT 5:   Review of AR, OR, IR, ER, UR.
DIRECTIONS: Say the name of the picture. Draw a circle around the letters that you hear in the name of the picture.

ar or ur	or ir ar	ar er or
er or ar	ar er or	ir or ar
ar or ir	or ur ar	er or ar
ur or ar	ar er or	or ar ir

94

DIRECTIONS: Read the sentence. Find the word at the bottom of the page that the sentence tells about. Print the correct word on the line.

1.   I use it when I eat.

2.   It is a safe place to play.

3.   It makes a nest in a tree.

4.   Mother's gray coat is made of it.

5.   He helps in the store.

6.   Little Boy Blue has one.

7.   Chickens and ducks live here.

8.   We get up at this time.

9.   A dog can do this.

10.   Mother has jam in it.

11.   We like to eat it.

12.   You can ride in it.

corn
yard
bird
fur

fork
horn
jar
morning

farm
car
clerk
bark

95

UNIT 6: Suffix -ING.
DIRECTIONS: In the first exercise, add the ending -ING to the root word. Print the new word. In the second exercise, complete the sentence by adding the ending -ING to the word in the column.

Add ing to these words.

sleep	_____	stay	_____
rent	_____	jump	_____
look	_____	play	_____
brush	_____	rock	_____
help	_____	start	_____
hunt	_____	fish	_____

Add ing and print the word in the space.

1. The children are _____ for the bus.   wait

2. Ann and Jean are _____ rope.   jump

3. Sue is _____ at the blue coat.   look

4. Jane is _____ Dick with the plates.   help

5. Mother is _____ Jane's hair   brush

6. The girls are _____ to help us.   stay

7. The boys went _____ in the lake.   fish

8. The baby is _____ in her crib.   sleep

UNIT 6: Suffixes -S and -ES.

DIRECTIONS: Choose the correct word, and print it on the line. Color one or two pictures in each box according to your answer. Sometimes you will color only one picture.

Words ending in X, Z, SS, SH, or CH usually add ES.

1. Dick broke a yellow

_____

dish   dishes

2. We have candy in two

_____

box   boxes

3. Did you see that shiny

_____ ?

star   stars

4. You drink milk from a

_____

glass   glasses

5. Do you use a hair

_____ ?

brush   brushes

6. She lost one red

_____

mitten   mittens

7. On the way home we saw two

_____

church   churches

8. Jack's mother gave him a

_____

cap   caps

9. "Peep, peep," said the two

_____

chick   chicks

10. Each year Mother cans

_____

peach   peaches

11. Billy went to see a

_____

dog   dogs

12. At the zoo we saw a

_____

seal   seals

UNIT 6: Suffix -ED.
DIRECTIONS: In the first exercise, add the ending -ED to the root word and print the new word on the line. In the second exercise, choose a word that you made in the first exercise to complete the sentences. In the third exercise, print the root word on the line.

Add ed to these words.

crack _____   help _____   pack _____

jump _____   kick _____   plant _____

rain _____   ask _____

Find the missing words.

1. Father _____ grass near the house.

2. Tim _____ the ball into the air.

3. The girls _____ rope after school.

4. Jack _____ nuts for the candy.

5. The boys _____ fix the desks.

6. Mother _____ my bag for the trip.

7. Pat _____ for a big red dog.

8. It _____ for two days.

Print the root word.

hunted _____   marched _____   bumped _____

asked _____   cleaned _____   painted _____

played _____   rained _____   passed _____

UNIT 6:   Review of suffixes -ES and -ED.
DIRECTIONS: Add either the ending -ES or the ending -ED to the root word to complete the
sentence. At the bottom of the page, add the ending -S or -ES to the root words
in the list and print them on the lines.

Add es or ed to the words.

1.   Jean brush_____ her hair until it shines.

2.   When Carlos miss_____ the bus, he walks.

3.   Ann ask _____ Mother to help her.

4.   The dog bark _____ when the car came near.

5.   It rain _____ all day Sunday.

6.   Rags jump_____ up to get the meat.

7.   Father fish _____ when we go to the beach.

8.   The boys play _____ ball in the schoolyard.

9.   Gym teach _____ us to keep fit.

Add s or es to the words.

| fish | branch | mail | hunt |
| buzz | help | pass | bump |

99

UNIT 6: Review of suffixes -S, -ES, -ED, and -ING.
DIRECTIONS: Draw a circle around the correct word to complete the sentence, and print it on the line.

1. Tom _____ the chickens.

feed
feeding
feeds

2. Day after day that truck _____ his house.

passes
passing
pass

3. A big boat was _____ on the lake.

floating
floats
floated

4. Mr. Gray went _____ for rabbits.

hunted
hunting
hunt

5. Jane will _____ to Grandmother.

reads
read
reading

6. He _____ faster than Billy and Dan.

work
working
worked

7. Ann was _____ Sue with her reading.

helped
helps
helping

8. Baby likes to go _____ .

walk
walks
walking

9. Mother _____ for her blue pen.

look
looking
looked

10. Joe went _____ with his father.

fished
fish
fishing

UNIT 6: TEST: Suffixes -S, -ES, -ED, and -ING.
DIRECTIONS: In the first exercise, make new words by adding the endings to the root words. In the second exercise, complete the sentence by adding the correct ending to the word in the column.

Add s, es, ed and ing to the words.

	s or es	ed	ing
bump			
mix			
help			
pass			
look			
clean			

Add an ending to the word, and print it on the line.

1. Father is _____ for the plant.   ask

2. We_____ rope this morning.   jump

3. It_____ until lunchtime.   rain

4. They are _____ to clean the desks.   go

5. We are_____ a good lunch.   pack

6. Mother _____ Mary Ann's hair.   braid

7. The boys_____ the pens to the girls.   pass

8. Mother _____ us to sing.   teach

UNIT 6:   Suffix -ING: doubling the final consonant.
DIRECTIONS: Add the ending -ING to the root word in the column, and complete the sentence.

When a short-vowel word ends in a single consonant, we usually double the consonant before adding ING.

1. The boys were _____ to the park.   run

2. Here comes a rabbit _____ in the grass.   hop

3. Mary is _____ her doll.   dress

4. Mother and I went _____ .   shop

5. She likes to go _____ in the lake.   swim

6. Tom's father is _____ for a deer.   hunt

7. The men are _____ the street.   clean

8. I saw a man _____ a big tree.   chop

9. John's dog is _____ for a bone.   beg

10. The boys are _____ near the lake.   camp

11. See the pony _____ down the road.   trot

12. Ted likes to go _____ with Father.   fish

13. The puppy is _____ in the box.   sit

14. Did you hear Timmy _____ the song?   hum

15. The rain is _____ off my hat.   drip

16. Mother is _____ me a glass of milk.   get

UNIT 6: Suffix -ED: doubling the final consonant.
DIRECTIONS: Add the ending -ED to the root word in the column, and complete the sentence. At the bottom of the page, make new words by adding the endings -ED and -ING to each word.

When a short-vowel word ends in a single consonant, we usually double the consonant before adding ED.

1. The little girl_____her doll.   hug

2. Jane_____to the little girl.   nod

3. Jack_____with his red boat.   play

4. Pat_____down the steps.   jump

5. The rabbit_____on the grass.   hop

6. Mary_____her mother for a bike.   beg

7. The big black dog_____his tail.   wag

8. Grandmother_____on the desk.   rap

9. Sue_____up her little yellow duck.   pick

10. Father_____the tree for us.   trim

11. Jane_____her hand into the pail.   dip

12. When the bell rang, we_____ printing.   stop

Add ed and ing to each word.

wag   **paint**   **hop**

UNIT 6:   Suffixes -ING and -ED: dropping final E.
DIRECTIONS: Add the ending -ING or -ED to the words and print the new words on the lines.
If a word ends with a silent E, drop the E before adding ING or ED.

DO NOT FORGET – If a word ends with a silent e, drop

the e and add ing or ed.

ing		ed	
hope		pave	
take		close	
get		joke	
make		bake	
eat		smile	
drive		save	
save		skate	
ride		hunt	
smoke		pile	
fade		wipe	
sit		use	
rain		hike	

DIRECTIONS: Recall the rules. In the first exercise, add the ending -ING to the root words.
In the second exercise, add the ending -ED to the root words.

Add ing and print the new word.

ride		fry	
rub		hide	
spin		fly	
frame		dig	
help		bite	
take		jump	
poke		whip	
hum		beg	

Add ed and print the new word.

pin		wag	
chase		rock	
print		hop	
dish		smoke	
play		scrub	
use		bake	
clap		drop	

UNIT 6: Review of suffixes -S, -ES, -ED, and -ING.
DIRECTIONS: Rewrite the word adding the ending that is above each column. At the bottom
of the page, add the correct ending to the root word to complete the sentence.

Remember your rules!

ing	ed	s or es
wave	smoke	peach
skate	pin	bird
drop	like	cross
smile	press	tree

Add an ending to the word, and print it on the line.

1. The children are _____ games.   play

2. My _____ is much better this year.   read

3. Father said that I may go _____.   swim

4. The old horse _____ down the road.   trot

5. Sally is _____ a birthday cake.   bake

6. The children are _____ on the ice.   skate

7. Grace is _____ us to sing.   teach

8. We _____ five boxes of stamps.   save

9. Mary is _____ her mother.   help

10. Mr. Gray is _____ the big bus.   drive

UNIT 6: Review of suffixes -S, -ES, -ED, and -ING.
DIRECTIONS: Add the correct ending to the words in the list, and use them to complete the sentences. At the bottom of the page, draw a box around the root word.

Add the correct ending to one of the words, and print it on the line.

ask	skate	cut	wax	drive
chop	rake	run	spell	drop

1. Mary Ann_____the words for me.

2. Last night, Jack_____ for a puppy.

3. I see children_____on the ice.

4. Joan is_____roses for Grandmother.

5. Jim is_____to the store for Mother.

6. Fred_____the yard each week.

7. Jack was in a hurry and_____his cap.

8. My mother_____the floor this morning.

9. My dad_____the blue car slowly.

10. The boys_____the trees down.

Draw a box around the root words.

dressed	buzzes	jumped	plays	puffed
brushing	crying	loading	boxes	dishes
cleaned	parking	wished	stayed	swimming
snapping	planned	cooking	drives	drops

107

UNIT 6: TEST: Suffixes -S, -ES, -ED, and -ING.
DIRECTIONS: Add the endings -ING, -S or -ES, and -ED to all the words.

	ing	s or es	ed
shine			
skate			
jump			
pass			
smile			
end			
play			
drop			
reach			
joke			
paint			
shop			
mix			

UNIT 6: Suffix -FUL.

DIRECTIONS: Add the ending -FUL to each root word to form a new word. Use the new words to complete the sentences. At the bottom of the page, draw a box around the root word.

hopeful

The ending is -ful.

The root word is hope.

care	_____	cheer	_____	play	_____
harm	_____	help	_____	thank	_____
pain	_____	rest	_____	fear	_____

Find the missing words.

1. Jack was _____ for his gifts.

2. Be _____ when you cross the street.

3. Tim had a _____ nap.

4. The _____ puppy begged for food.

5. The bad tooth was _____ .

6. The _____ children cleaned the desks.

Draw a box around the root word.

| painful | hopeful | restful | grateful |
| thankful | cheerful | playful | careful |

109

UNIT 6: Suffixes -LESS and -NESS.

DIRECTIONS: Choose the correct word from the list, and complete the sentences. At the bottom of the page, add the ending -LESS to the words in the first column and add the ending -NESS to the words in the second column.

Find the missing words.

| careless | darkness | thickness | sickness | neatness |
| harmless | leafless | homeless | hopeless | boneless |

1. When the storm came, the _____ scared us.

2. "He will not bite you," said Tom. "Spot is _____."

3. Ray was _____ and lost his books.

4. _____ kept Ted out of school for three weeks.

5. The _____ of his coat kept him from getting hurt.

6. The little lost dog was _____.

7. Winter came at last, and the trees were _____.

8. Joe says he likes to eat fish if it is _____.

9. Miss King gave Ellen a good grade in _____.

10. It was _____ to try to fix the boat.

Add less		Add ness	
home	_____	good	_____
hope	_____	sad	_____
care	_____	soft	_____
sleep	_____	sick	_____

UNIT 6: Suffix -LY.
DIRECTIONS: Add the ending -LY to the root word, and print the new word on the line. In the sentences at the bottom of the page, draw a circle around the words having the ending -LY. Print the root word on the line.

quickly

The ending is -ly.

The root word is quick.

glad		near	
hard		swift	
soft		brave	
neat		cruel	
wise		sweet	

Draw a circle around the words ending in ly, and print the root word on the line.

1. The children worked quickly.

2. The fireman acted bravely.

3. Mary was playing the music softly.

4. The king spoke wisely.

5. The wicked king acted cruelly.

6. The little girls sang sweetly.

7. The boys will gladly help.

8. The wagon was painted neatly.

111

UNIT 6: Review of suffixes -S, -ES, -ED, -ING, -LY, and -FUL.
DIRECTIONS: Add the correct ending to the words in the list to make them mean more than one.
At the bottom of the page, draw a box around the root words.

Make the words mean more than one.

desk	_____	match	_____
box	_____	glass	_____
wish	_____	queen	_____
patch	_____	lunch	_____
dog	_____	stove	_____
game	_____	train	_____
book	_____	doll	_____
can	_____	bench	_____
bag	_____	dish	_____
church	_____	school	_____
brush	_____	peach	_____

Draw a box around the root words.

sleeping	looking	gladly	toasted
rubbing	folded	quickly	sweetly
cupful	swiftly	painted	hopping
slowly	printing	harmful	planted

UNIT 6: Review of suffixes -LY, -FUL, -LESS, and -NESS.
DIRECTIONS: In each box, match the root word in the first column with the new word in the second column. Print the correct number on the line.

_____ quick	1. slowly	_____ glad	1. softly
_____ sweet	2. quickly	_____ soft	2. nearly
_____ slow	3. sweetly	_____ near	3. lovely
_____ loud	4. loudly	_____ love	4. gladly
_____ use	1. playful	_____ help	1. armful
_____ play	2. handful	_____ hope	2. hopeful
_____ cheer	3. useful	_____ arm	3. helpful
_____ hand	4. cheerful	_____ cup	4. cupful
_____ home	1. cheerless	_____ care	1. fearless
_____ use	2. homeless	_____ sleeve	2. jobless
_____ wire	3. useless	_____ fear	3. careless
_____ cheer	4. wireless	_____ job	4. sleeveless
_____ like	1. sweetness	_____ good	1. softness
_____ sad	2. sickness	_____ dark	2. nearness
_____ sweet	3. likeness	_____ near	3. darkness
_____ sick	4. sadness	_____ soft	4. goodness

UNIT 6:   Review of suffixes -LY, -FUL, -LESS, and -NESS.
DIRECTIONS: Use one of the endings to correctly complete each sentence. At the bottom of the
page, choose a word from the list that means the same as the words in the
column.

Add an ending to the words.

ly   ful   less   ness

1. Jane is a very friend_____ girl.

2. It is care _____ to leave toys on the steps.

3. Our puppy is very play_____.

4. Our car stopped when we were near_____ home.

5. The old man safe_____ crossed the street.

6. Little children should be help _____.

7. Laugh and play your sad _____ away.

8. We like boys and girls who are cheer_____.

Find the word that means the same.

homeless   colorful   quickly   harmful

sadly   safely   playful   helpful

1. full of color _____   5. full of play _____

2. no home _____   6. being of help _____

3. with harm _____   7. with speed _____

4. with sadness _____   8. in a safe way _____

·IRECTIONS: Add the ending, and print the new word on the line. At the bottom of the page,
add the correct ending to the root word and use the new word to complete the
sentence.

Add the ending, and print the new word.

ly

soft

glad

nice

ful

play

help

cheer

less

home

spot

pain

ness

sad

sick

dark

Add the ending to the root word, and print it on the line.

play   1. Spot is a very_____puppy.

home   2. The little kitten was_____.

cheer   3. The sick boy was very_____.

glad   4. Mark will_____help you.

dark   5. We were in_____after the storm.

glass   6. Drink this_____of milk.

neat   7. She does her work_____.

DIRECTIONS: Add the endings -ER and -EST to each word, and print the new words on the lines.
At the bottom of the page, draw pictures to show the meaning of each word.

Add <u>er</u> and <u>est</u> to each word.

near

long

fast

dark

mean

thick

safe

sort

late

Draw a picture for these words.

long	longer	longest
thick	thicker	thickest

116

UNIT 6: Suffixes -ER and -EST: words ending in Y.
DIRECTIONS: At the top of the page, add the endings -ER and -EST to the words in the list.
At the bottom of the page, complete the sentences by adding -ER and -EST to the root word.

When a word ends in Y after a consonant, change the Y to I before adding the ending -ER or -EST.

Add <u>er</u> and <u>est</u> to each word.

silly

sleepy

windy

happy

funny

Add <u>er</u> or <u>est</u> to the word, and print it on the line.

1. The _____ thing happened today.   funny

2. You are much _____ than you were.   happy

3. That is the _____ dog I have ever seen.   lazy

4. The blue dress is _____ than the red one.   pretty

5. He was the _____ man in the circus.   jolly

6. Tom tried to tell the _____ story.   silly

7. We must wait for a _____ day to sail.   windy

8. This road is _____ than the one we were on.   bumpy

9. Sally was the _____ one at the State Fair.   lucky

10. Look for the _____ can you can find.   rusty

117

UNIT 6: Suffix -ES: words ending in Y.
DIRECTIONS: Read the sentence and think of the rule. Print the new word on the line.

When a word ends in Y after a consonant, change the Y to I before adding the ending -ES.

daisy   cherry   lily

daisies   cherries   lilies

1. Joe liked the five little circus_____.   pony

2. Miss Day asked us to make two_____ of our work.   copy

3. There were three_____in the box.   bunny

4. We picked a bunch of _____.   daisy

5. We liked the two black_____best.   puppy

6. Dad told us two _____.   story

7. Mother was speaking to all the_____.   lady

8. The lady gave Bill ten_____.   penny

9. Did you pick this box of_____?   cherry

UNIT 6: Suffix -ES: words ending in Y.
DIRECTIONS: Change the words to mean more than one. In the sentences, choose the correct word and print it on the line. Print the names of the pictures at the bottom of the page.

Add es to the words, and write them on the lines.

lady _____   city _____   pony _____

cherry _____   daisy _____   jelly _____

study _____   lily _____   bunny _____

dress _____   box _____   candy _____

Print the correct word on the line.

1. Mary went to two birthday (party - parties).

2. We like to hear you read a (story - stories).

3. Ted has fifty (penny - pennies) in the bank.

4. I see a (cherry - cherries) on the dish.

5. Some (baby - babies) smile and play all day.

6. There are pretty (lily - lilies) in the vase.

Print the names of the pictures.

UNIT 6: Suffix -ES: words ending in Y.
DIRECTIONS: Read the sentence, and print the new word on the line to complete the sentence.

1. We have to read five new_____.   story

2. The two helpful_____ran away.   fairy

3. Jack picked some ripe_____.   cherry

4. Two_____got on the bus.   lady

5. Susan went to three_____.   party

6. Cindy planted six pots of_____.   lily

7. The boy spent his ten_____.   penny

8. Can you name some big_____?   city

9. It is fun to pick_____.   berry

10. Jane and Ann looked for_____.   daisy

11. Three_____live on this farm.   family

12. The robin is feeding her_____.   baby

13. Mother got some white_____.   dish

14. At the store we saw five_____.   bunny

15. The_____trotted up the road.   pony

UNIT 6: Suffixes -ES and -ED: words ending in Y.
DIRECTIONS: At the top of the page, add the endings -ES and -ED to the words in the list. At the bottom of the page, complete the sentences by adding the endings -ES or -ED to the root word.

When a word ends in Y after a consonant, change the Y to I before adding the ending -ES or -ED.

Change these words to fit the correct ending.

	es	ed
spy		
fry		
study		
dry		
try		
empty		

Add es or ed to the word, and print it on the line.

1. Last year Joe _____ to get good grades.   try

2. The rich man was_____ by the tramp.   pity

3. The baby _____ when it is hot.   cry

4. Ruth _____ her numbers last week.   study

5. The wind has _____ the wet dresses.   dry

6. An airplane _____ up in the sky.   fly

7. Last Sunday Mother _____ chicken for us.   fry

8. This morning Jack _____ the basket.   empty

9. Dan _____ home this morning.   hurry

UNIT 6:   TEST: Suffixes -ER, -EST, -ES, and -ED: words ending in Y.
DIRECTIONS: On the lines, print the root words for the words that are underlined in the
              sentences. Change the words at the bottom of the page to mean more than one.

Print the root word on the line.

1. My doll sleeps and <u>cries</u>.

2. Father <u>tried</u> to shut the gate.

3. Sunday was <u>sunnier</u> than Thursday.

4. He was the <u>happiest</u> boy there.

5. This rope is <u>longer</u>.

6. Jack and I <u>studied</u> very hard.

7. The man has two <u>ponies</u> on his farm.

8. Mother tells us many <u>stories</u>.

9. This is the <u>biggest</u> tree in town.

10. Grandmother <u>fried</u> the eggs for me.

Change <u>y</u> to <u>i</u> and add <u>es</u>. Print the new word on the line.

candy _____   baby _____

berry _____   puppy _____

lady _____   pony _____

fairy _____   cooky _____

UNIT 6:   Contractions in which WILL is shortened.
DIRECTIONS: On the line, print the word that means the same as the two words given. At the
bottom of the page, print the shortened form of the two underlined words in each
sentence.

she will   she'll

She'll is the short way of writing she will.

Find the one word that means the same.

1.   2.

I will   _____   you'll

we will   _____   they'll

she will   _____   she'll

he will   _____   we'll

they will   _____   I'll

you will   _____   he'll

Print the one word that means the same.

1. I will go to the store with you.   _____

2. He will mail the letters   _____

3. She will read the story now.   _____

4. We will play games with Tom.   _____

5. They will plant the tree.   _____

6. You will have a surprise this week.   _____

UNIT 6: Contractions in which NOT is shortened.
DIRECTIONS: On the line, print the word in column 2 that means the same as the two words
             in column 1. At the bottom of the page, print the two words that mean the
             same as the underlined word.

can not   can't

Can't is the short way of writing can not.

Find the one word that means the same.

do not _____ can't

will not _____ didn't

is not _____ weren't

can not _____ isn't

are not _____ couldn't

did not _____ aren't

were not _____ don't

could not _____ won't

Print the two words on the line.

1. I can't go to the park today. _____

2. Jane isn't going with you. _____

3. We haven't a big box. _____

4. Tim didn't clean the yard. _____

5. Ann doesn't need her coat. _____

124

UNIT 6:   Contractions in which IS or HAVE is shortened.
DIRECTIONS: On the line, print the two words that mean the same as the shortened form. At the bottom of the page, print the shortened form of the two underlined words in each sentence.

Print the two words on the line.

is

1. he's
2. that's
3. it's
4. she's
5. there's

have

1. I've
2. you've
3. we've
4. they've
5. I've

Print the one word that means the same.

1. There is a big fire in the town.

2. You have never been late for school.

3. It is fun to swim in the lake.

4. I have seen a rainbow.

5. He is smiling at the funny joke.

6. We have been to the game.

7. That is the rule for the game.

8. She is trying to print her name.

9. They have a color TV set.

UNIT 6: Contractions in which AM, ARE, or US is shortened.
DIRECTIONS: On the line, print the word that means the same as the two words. At the bottom of the page, print the two words that mean the same as the underlined word in each sentence.

Print the one word that means the same.

you are   _____   we are   _____

I am   _____   you are   _____

let us   _____   I am   _____

we are   _____   they are   _____

they are   _____   let us

Print the two words that mean the same.

1. We're going to pick some buds.   _____

2. They're in the tree.   _____

3. Let's go in a bus.   _____

4. I'm going to take a basket.   _____

5. You're going with me.   _____

6. "They're mine," Tom cried.   _____

7. I'm not the one.   _____

8. We're not to take it.   _____

9. You're the one he asked for.   _____

UNIT 6: Review of contractions.
DIRECTIONS: Print the number of each shortened form in the space in front of the two words that have the same meaning. Then complete the sentences.

Match the words.

1. we're   _____ I am   9. don't   _____ is not
2. you'll   _____ we are   10. she's   _____ you are
3. it's   _____ will not   11. you're   _____ I will
4. can't   _____ he is   12. isn't   _____ we will
5. I'm   _____ you will   13. she'll   _____ do not
6. he's   _____ let us   14. we'll   _____ I have
7. won't   _____ can not   15. I'll   _____ she will
8. let's   _____ it is   16. I've   _____ she is

Find the missing word.

1. Please_____stay out today.
   isn't   don't   won't

2. The baby_____walk very well.
   isn't   can't   don't

3. I will help you if_____let me.
   you'll   it's   we'll

4. Mother said, "_____go downtown."
   I'll   won't   she's

UNIT 6: Review of contractions.
DIRECTIONS: On the line, print the shortened form of the two words that are underlined in each
sentence.

1. Tom <u>can not</u> come to school today.

2. <u>He will</u> read a story to the class.

3. <u>Let us</u> start the game.

4. <u>You are</u> very helpful.

5. Jane <u>has not</u> missed a day of school.

6. <u>I am</u> going home now.

7. Someday <u>we will</u> play in the rain.

8. <u>He is</u> feeling well today.

9. <u>I have</u> a new green brush to use.

10. <u>I will</u> help you if you will let me.

11. Jean <u>can not</u> skate very well.

12. <u>It is</u> time to go to school.

13. We <u>do not</u> have time to stay.

14. Ann <u>will not</u> wait for the girls.

15. Jack <u>is not</u> going to play with us.

UNIT 6: TEST: Contractions.
DIRECTIONS: On the line, print the shortened form of the two words that are underlined in each sentence. At the bottom of the page, print the two words that mean the same as the shortened form.

Print the one word that means the same.

1. I am six years old today.

2. You are a good reader.

3. We do not like to be late.

4. You will have to hurry.

5. Tom would not tell a lie.

6. We are going to school.

7. Let us do our work.

8. She will take care of Timmy.

9. There is your school bus.

10. I have a story to tell you.

Print the two words that mean the same.

I've _____   it's _____

he'll _____   didn't _____

they're _____   you've _____

she's _____   let's _____

isn't _____   won't _____

UNIT 6:   TEST: Contractions.
DIRECTIONS: Print the shortened form that means the same as the two words. At the bottom
of the page, draw a circle around the correct word and print it on the line.

Print the one word that means the same.

I will	_____	is not	_____
I am	_____	can not	_____
it is	_____	we will	_____
I have	_____	he is	_____
do not	_____	could not	_____
let us	_____	there is	_____

Draw a circle around the missing word, and print it on the line.

1. _____ happy to be here.   I'm   There's

2. _____ a surprise for Mother.   Didn't   It's

3. _____ my new bike.   That's   Isn't

4. Pat _____ be here today.   won't   it's

5. _____ a new reader.   I'll   I've

6. Jack _____ get in the game.   didn't   it's

7. _____ the first one here.   Let's   You're

8. _____ my best work.   That's   Won't

9. He _____ need my help.   aren't   doesn't

130

DIRECTIONS: Read the sentences. Find the word in the list that each sentence tells about, and print it on the line.

If a one-part word (or syllable) has two vowels, the first vowel is usually long and the second one is silent.

chain	stain	mailman	snail
nail	rain	hair	paint
chair	train	pail	sail

Find the missing words.

1. I ride on railroad tracks. _____

2. I bring letters to your home. _____

3. You put water in me. _____

4. I make you put on a raincoat. _____

5. You can sit on me. _____

6. I am made of many links. _____

7. Girls like to curl me. _____

8. I am on a boat. _____

9. I am an ink spot on a dress. _____

10. I live in the water. _____

UNIT 7: Regular double vowels EE and EA.
DIRECTIONS: Complete the sentence by using the words in the list. In the box at the end of each
line, print the two vowels in the word that contain the long sound of A or E.

Find the missing word, and print it on the line. Then print the two
vowels that give the long sound of <u>a</u> or <u>e</u>.

| green | pail | say | see | train | read | mailman |
| rain | feed | street | away | tree | meat | team |

1. The pigs ran _____ in a hurry. ☐

2. We _____ friends at school. ☐

3. Patty likes to _____ this story. ☐

4. The _____ comes from the sky. ☐

5. The grass is _____ in the spring. ☐

6. The _____ had a letter for me. ☐

7. Look before you cross the _____. ☐

8. The dog ran away with the _____. ☐

9. What did Mother _____ to you? ☐

10. It was fun to _____ the peeps. ☐

11. The baseball _____ played hard. ☐

12. Jack and Jill had a _____. ☐

13. The _____ made its first trip. ☐

14. This _____ has ripe peaches. ☐

UNIT 7:   Regular double vowels OA, IE, and OE.
DIRECTIONS: Print the number of the picture in the correct box. At the bottom of the page, draw a circle around the correct word and print it on the line.

Print the number of the picture in the correct box.

☐ hoe ☐ soap ☐ tie ☐ toad ☐ pie ☐ coal ☐ road ☐ boat

1
3
5
7
2
4
6
8

Draw a circle around the missing word, and print it on the line.

1. Jim's dog likes to eat _____ .   met   meat   make

2. Joe cut his little _____ .   hoe   load   toe

3. My father likes his _____ .   tie   die   lie

4. See my red _____ .   catch   came   coat

5. Mother baked a peach _____ .   tie   pie   die

6. It's fun to ride in a _____ .   bat   boat   goat

7. Get a bar of _____ .   soak   seek   soap

8. Spot ran down the _____ .   rod   road   ride

9. Jill _____ the string.   cried   tied   died

UNIT 7:   Review of regular double vowels AI, AY, EE, EA, OA, IE, and OE.
DIRECTIONS: Draw a circle around the correct word to complete the sentence, and print it on the
line. At the bottom of the page, print the correct regular double vowel in the
space in each sentence.

Find the missing word.

1. Hear the frogs_____.   coat   croak   coal

2. Mother baked a_____.   tie   pie   die

3. Billy won a _____ bike.   green   grab   grass

4. The pepper made me _____.   steal   sneeze   spear

5. This boat will_____far.   sail   pail   tail

6. Father will_____the gate.   faint   train   paint

7. The farmer lost a_____.   weep   sheep   deep

Add ea, oa, ee, ai, ay, or ie.

1. Billy Goat, do not eat my c_____t.

2. A dog can't go up a tr_____.

3. I just had t_____st and milk.

4. It is a very cl_____r day.

5. Bill, may I keep your pen all d_____?

6. I use s_____p when I take a bath.

7. Bill broke the ch_____n.

8. Do you like to eat p_____?

UNIT 7:   Review of regular double vowels AI, AY, EE, EA, OA, IE, and OE.

DIRECTIONS: From the list at the bottom of the page, choose the name of each picture and print it on the line.

rain	hoe	pie	beet	beads	hay	tree
leaf	deer	boat	daisy	Joe	nails	feet

135

DIRECTIONS: Print the number of the correct answer in the box. Answer the riddles at the bottom of the page by adding beginning and ending letters when you need them.

Find the missing word, and print the number in the box.

The farmer feeds the ☐ .   1. soap

Tom's boat can ☐ on the lake.   2. sheep

A ☐ is used to dig.   3. hay

Mother said, "Use ☐ on your hands."   4. float

Baby ☐ when she broke her doll.   5. hoe

Jack picked a ripe ☐ from the tree.   6. pie

Mother made a blackberry ☐ .   7. paint

Father had to ☐ the house.   8. cried

Farmer Gray put the ☐ in the barn.   9. peach

Answer the riddles. Add the beginning and ending letters when you need them.

1. It fell from the tree.   _____ ea _____

2. It is something to put on.   _____ oa _____

3. A dog wags it.   _____ ai _____

4. Horses like to eat it.   _____ ay _____

5. It is something we can eat.   _____ ee _____

6. Mother bakes it for us.   _____ ie _____

7. They help us stand.   _____ ee _____

UNIT 7: Regular double vowel OW (as in SNOW).

DIRECTIONS: Print the correct name under each picture. At the bottom of the page, choose the correct word and print it on the line.

Print the name of the picture.

_____	_____	_____
_____	_____	_____

snow   rainbow   snowman   crow   bow   bowl

Find the missing word.

1. The wind began to _____ .   bow   blow

2. Jane played in the _____ .   snow   slow

3. We must not paint too _____ .   row   slow

4. Pass the _____ of fruit.   bowl   bow

5. A _____ is a black bird.   grow   crow

6. Can you _____ the stone?   throw   grow

137

UNIT 7: Irregular double vowel OO (as in ROOSTER, SCHOOL).
DIRECTIONS: Draw a circle around the correct word, and print it on the line.

Choose the correct word, and print it on the line.

1. May I sweep the _____ ?   moon   shoot   room

2. A rooster likes _____ .   fool   stool   food

3. Betty swept with a _____ .   soon   broom   boom

4. The _____ roof is black.   tool   spool   school

5. Jack had a loose _____ .   tooth   spoon   broom

6. Tom swam in the _____ .   cool   pool   tool

7. The lake water was _____ .   stool   spool   cool

8. At _____ we eat lunch.   spoon   noon   moon

9. Mary sat on the _____ .   pool   stool   cool

10. The baby ate with a _____ .   spoon   broom   soon

11. Father took us to the _____ .   too   zoo   moo

12. If it rains you must wear your _____ .   boat   boost   boots

13. Father is looking for his _____ .   tools   fools   drools

14. We saw a _____ at the farm.   soothe   goose   boom

15. That bill is _____ much.   too   zoo   boo

16. Mother bought a _____ of white thread.   soon   spool   stool

138

UNIT 7: Irregular double vowel OO (as in BOOK, HOOD).
DIRECTIONS: In the exercise at the top of the page, draw a circle around the correct word and print it on the line. At the bottom of the page, print two rhyming words.

Find the missing words.

1. Tim _____ the plum tree.   look   shook   hook

2. Will you chop the _____ ?   wood   hood   took

3. We can wade in the _____ .   book   cook   brook

4. I will _____ for Jane.   look   nook   crook

5. Bob _____ out his books.   good   took   stood

6. Put the coat on the _____ .   hook   look   shook

7. Show the _____ to Sue.   look   good   book

8. Sam _____ up and looked.   took   stood   good

9. A _____ boy will do it.   good   wood   crook

10. See the _____ on my coat.   cook   hood   look

Print the name of the picture and a rhyming word.

139

DIRECTIONS: Find the correct word, and complete the sentences. At the bottom of the page, draw a circle around the correct word.

Find the missing words.

1. Sally _____ the book last week.   bread

2. Sometimes the _____ is cold, sometimes it is hot. read

3. Mother needs _____ for supper.   leather

4. My purse is made of _____ .   ready

5. Are you _____ for school?   sweater

6. Grandmother needed more _____ .   breath

7. Tom fell and bumped his _____ .   thread

8. It is cool so you need a _____ .   head

9. My red hen lost a _____   weather

10. When it is cold you can see your_____   feather

Draw a circle around the correct word.

1. In the morning you eat (breading, breakfast, breathing).

2. In the big, green (sweater, weather, meadow) we saw the sheep.

3. Everyone has a (head, bread, thread).

4. The (feather, weather, leather) today is cool.

5. Mother uses (feathers, cleanser, bread) to clean the tub.

UNIT 7: Review of regular and irregular double vowels.
DIRECTIONS: Print the number of the answer in the box in front of each riddle. At the bottom of the page, draw a circle around the name of the picture.

Print the numbers in the boxes.

☐ Something Mother uses for sweeping.		1. bread
☐ A food we can eat with each meal.		2. blow
☐ Something we read in school.		3. sweater
☐ You can do this to a horn.		4. broom
☐ Something that shines when it is dark.		5. book
☐ Something to put on when it is cool.		6. spread
☐ Something for a bed.		7. stool
☐ Something we see during winter.		8. rooster
☐ Something to sit on.		9. moon
☐ A bird that crows.		10. snow

Draw a circle around the name of the picture.

headstone headline deadline	stool spoon moon	cleanser weather sweater	stool pool tool
bread read thread	peaches peacock peaceful	moon broom booth	feather leather father

141

DIRECTIONS: Find the correct word and complete the sentence. At the bottom of the page, draw a circle around the two vowels in each word that make one sound. Print them on the line.

Find the missing word.

1.   Did you _____ the dinner?

book   cool   cook

2.   There was a _____ of candy on the tray.

boot   bowl   howl

3.   When Tom fell he bumped his _____.

head   heap   lead

4.   The children begged to swim in the _____.

pool   wool   poor

5.   These men eat lunch at _____.

room   roof   noon

6.   The boys took the _____ stone across the road.

heavy   lead   leave

Draw a circle around the two vowels in the words that make one sound.
Print the two letters on the line.

root _____   yellow _____   bean _____   leap _____   row _____

moon _____   hoop _____   tea _____   float _____   dead _____

leave _____   coat _____   slow _____   book _____   meat _____

bow _____   team _____   wood _____   tool _____   zoo _____

bread _____   bowl _____   peach _____   room _____   pillow _____

UNIT 7:   Irregular double vowels AU and AW.
DIRECTIONS: Find the correct word and print it on the line.

| saw | auto | paw |

1. The dog gave me his _____.   fawn

2. The crow said, "_____."   draw

3. I helped Father cut the green _____.   Caw

4. A baby deer is a _____.   saw

5. Sally will _____ a snowman.   paw

6. Baby can _____ on the floor.   lawn

7. I cut the wood with a _____.   claws

8. The bird can scratch with its _____.   laws

9. We drink milk with a _____.   because

10. The boys rode in an old _____.   straw

11. We must obey the _____.   crawl

12. Jill ran away _____ of the snake.   auto

UNIT 7: Irregular double vowels AU and AW.

DIRECTIONS: Read the sentence, and print the correct word on the line. The words in the balloons will help you.

1. Lions like to eat _____ meat.

2. The man said, "Keep off the _____."

3. _____ was the boy with a new wagon.

4. The hawk held the chick in its _____.

5. Father will _____ away the rocks.

6. I will now _____ a picture of you.

7. Sometimes we _____ when we speak.

8. When we are sleepy we _____.

9. Baby is just starting to _____.

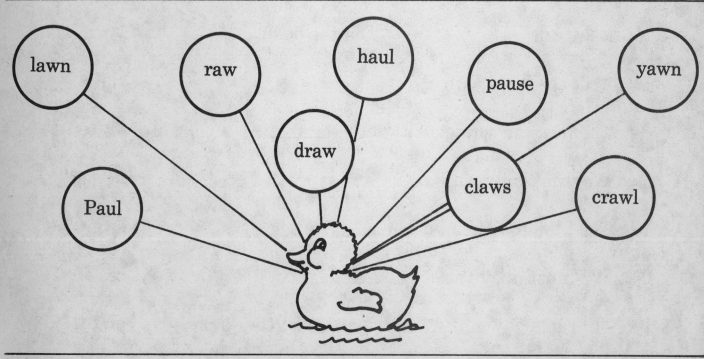

lawn raw haul pause yawn draw Paul claws crawl

144

DIRECTIONS: Complete the sentences making use of words from the list. At the bottom of the page, print the name of the picture on the line.

Find the missing words. _____

1. We get wool from _____.   gray

2. The milk for the kitten was in the _____.   bread

3. We read a good story in _____ today.   peas

4. We planted _____ in the garden.   woods

5. Mother needed some _____ for dinner.   raining

6. I gave Father a red _____.   sheep

7. See those oak trees in the _____.   bowl

8. Mary has a _____ coat.   peach

9. I put on my rubbers when it is _____.   school

10. Jean ate a _____ with her lunch.   tie

Print the name of the picture on the line.

_____   _____   _____   _____

UNIT 7:   TEST: Double vowels.
DIRECTIONS: Complete the sentences making use of the correct word from the list.

train	cried	peach	pain	read
crow	rooster	sail	play	green
books	bread	lawn	Please	cheeks

1. Mother gave Jane a big _____ to eat.

2. Baby likes to _____ with her doll.

3. The little red _____ stopped on the track.

4. Tom _____ when he fell.

5. Baby has nice pink _____ .

6. Jack _____ ten books last summer.

7. Pat can _____ his new yellow boat.

8. The red _____ woke us up this morning.

9. The black _____ rested in the tree.

10. Children like to look at funny _____ .

11. We ate _____ and jelly for lunch.

12. Jim had a _____ in his side.

13. _____ , may I pet the monkey?

14. The grass is pretty and _____ .

146

UNIT 8: Diphthongs OU and OW.

DIRECTIONS: Look at the picture. Say its name. Find its name in the list of words, and print the number of the word in the box. Color the pictures.

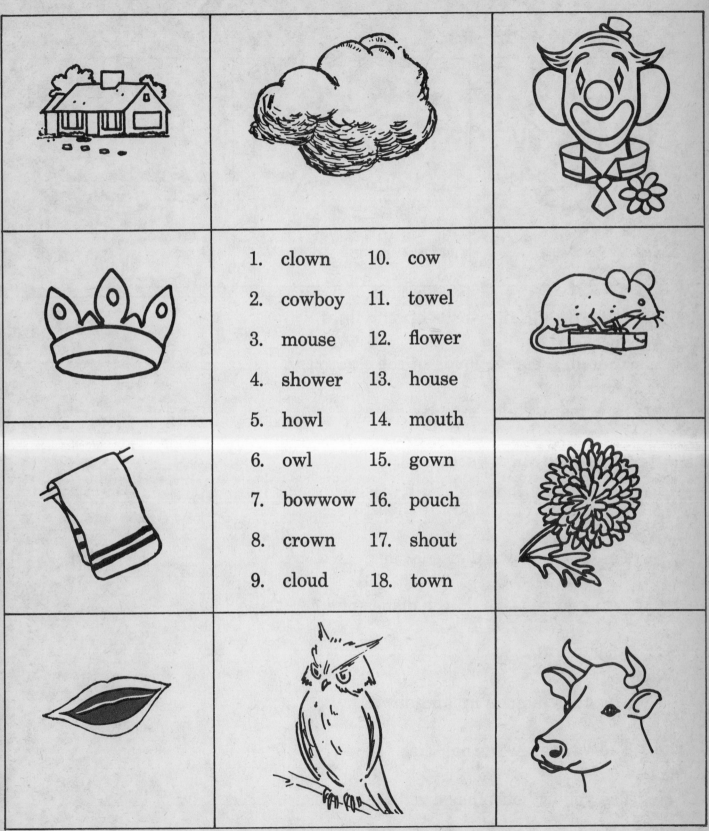

1. clown   10. cow
2. cowboy 11. towel
3. mouse   12. flower
4. shower 13. house
5. howl   14. mouth
6. owl   15. gown
7. bowwow 16. pouch
8. crown   17. shout
9. cloud   18. town

UNIT 8: Diphthongs OU and OW.
DIRECTIONS: Look at the picture. Say its name, and then notice how its name is spelled. At the
bottom of the page, find the OU and the OW words in the sentences and print them
on the lines.

Say the names of the pictures.

crown

cow

cloud

Print the <u>ow</u> and <u>ou</u> words on the lines.

1.   There are many clouds in the sky today.

2.   How many children played games?

3.   The birds will fly south.

4.   The car went around the block.

5.   The funny clown danced a jig.

6.   Will you help me do the dishes now?

7.   Dick is a Boy Scout.

8.   The boys jumped up and down.

9.   The owl sat in the oak tree.

10. The yellow house has a red roof.

UNIT 8: Review of diphthongs OU and OW.
DIRECTIONS: Read each riddle. Find the correct answer in the list of words at the top of the page, and print it on the line.

owl   cow   house   clown   flower   cloud   plow   ground

1. I am in the sky.

   Sometimes I bring you rain.

   What am I? _____

   ----

2. I am in the garden.

   I am very colorful.

   Maybe I grow in your yard, too. _____

   What am I? -----------------

3. I am wide awake in the dark.

   I hoot and howl.

   What am I? _____

   ----

4. You stay in me.

   I keep the wind and rain from you.

   What am I? _____

   ----

5. You can plant seeds in me.

   The farmer must plow me.

   What am I? _____

   ----

6. I have a funny suit.

   I do many tricks.

   I can make you smile. _____

   What am I? -----------------

7. You can see me at the farm.

   I eat green grass.

   I give you good milk. _____

   What am I? -----------------

8. The farmer uses me.

   I help him make his garden.

   What am I? _____

149

UNIT 8: The two sounds of OW.
DIRECTIONS: Look at the words. If the OW has the sound of long O, print an X on the line.
At the bottom of the page, find the OW words and print them on the line.

Mark an X on the line if it has the sound of long o.

_____ how	_____ snow	_____ gown
_____ own	_____ town	_____ crowd
_____ now	_____ bowl	_____ grow
_____ low	_____ plow	_____ power
_____ owl	_____ slow	_____ flow
_____ know	_____ show	_____ brown
_____ crow	_____ crown	_____ down

Print the ow words on the lines.

1. The clown fell off the big box.   1. _____

2. Ann had a pink bow in her hair.   2. _____

3. The cowboy rode a white horse.   3. _____

4. Mary cut the pretty flower.   4. _____

5. Jim went downtown.   5. _____

6. Can you eat a bowl of popcorn?   6. _____

UNIT 8: Diphthongs OI and OY.
DIRECTIONS: Draw a circle around the word that describes the picture. Complete the sentences
at the bottom of the page.

Draw a circle around the name of the picture.

boy	boy	corn
boil	rag	coil
bill	rug	coins
bell	toy	come
sail	oak	toil
Sally	oil	tail
sell	open	too
soil	out	toys
paint	noise	came
penny	nail	cot
point	near	coil
pan	nose	coin

Find the missing words.

1. The _____ train is in the big box.   oil

2. This train needs _____ to make it run.   coins

3. The _____ likes this ball best of all.   boy

4. I have _____ in my purse.   toy

151

DIRECTIONS: Read the story. Draw a circle around the OI words, and a box around the OY words. Then answer the questions at the bottom of the page.

The Little Toy Train

There was a little boy named Roy. His father gave him a toy train for his birthday. This made Roy a very happy little boy.

Roy took very good care of his toy train. Each time he used the train he oiled it. This made the toy train go fast.

But one day Roy oiled it too much. The toy train went faster and faster. It went so fast that Roy could not catch it.

Mother was in the kitchen broiling meat. The toy train went out to her. But she could not catch it.

Roy chased the toy train out the back door and down the path. But he could not catch it.

Baby was sitting on the grass. The toy train went to her and stopped. Baby was very happy. "Now I have a toy train," she said as she picked it up.

Roy said, "Baby, you have my toy train. It ran away from me. I used too much oil."

Baby gave Roy his toy train.

"Thank you, Baby," said Roy. "I will not spoil my toy train again by oiling it too much. From now on I will be more careful."

1. What was the little boy's name?

2. What did he get for his birthday?

3. What made the train go so fast?

4. Who picked up the toy train?

5. Did Roy get his toy train back?

UNIT 8: Diphthongs OI and OY.
DIRECTIONS: Find the correct word, and complete the sentences.

Find the missing words.

1. Mary Ann will not _____ her new book.   point   spoil   said

2. Do not put _____ near the fire.   boil   laid   oil

3. I am going to _____ the Boy Scouts.   joint   join   jail

4. You must not let the milk _____.   boil   bail   oil

Find the missing words.

1. A pencil has a _____.

2. Father puts _____ in his car.

3. The water is _____ on the stove.

4. The _____ said, "Come join the fun."

5. The baby made _____ with the drum.

6. The _____ boat has a big sail.

toy   boiling   oil   point   noise   boys

153

DIRECTIONS: Answer each question by printing "yes" or "no" on the line. At the bottom of
the page, complete each sentence by finding the correct word in the list.

Print yes or no on the line.

1. Is a penny a coin?

2. Is Ann a boy's name?

3. Can you play with a toy horn?

4. Is oil used in a car?

5. Is a point the same as paint?

6. Can Mother boil water for tea?

Find the missing words.

1. Mother will _____ the eggs for lunch.   coins

2. The _____ was kind to the lost dog.   toy

3. Jim has three _____ to spend.   boil

4. _____ helped his dad weed the yard.   Roy

5. The baby found the _____ in the box.   point

6. A pin has a sharp _____ on it.   boy

UNIT 8:   Diphthong EW.
DIRECTIONS: Complete each sentence by finding the correct word in the list. At the bottom of
the page, print two words that rhyme with each of the words you find there.

Find the missing words.

1. Sally scored a _____ points in the game.   screw

2. Each time I _____ the stick Pal got it.   few

3. The little kitten said, " _____ ."   grew

4. Mother said, "Please _____ your food."   new

5. You have a pretty _____ dress.   chew

6. The grass was wet with _____ .   flew

7. Many flowers _____ in the garden.   Mew

8. Mother made _____ for dinner.   drew

9. He needs one more _____ to fix it.   dew

10. The wind _____ the trees down.   blew

11. Dick _____ funny faces.   threw

12. A crow _____ into our yard.   stew

Print rhyming words.

few   screw   drew

_____   _____   _____

_____   _____   _____

155

UNIT 8:   Diphthong EW.
DIRECTIONS: Draw a circle around the correct word.

1. Sue has a (new, drew, grew) pink dress.

2. The red flowers (few, chew, grew) in the garden.

3. Grandmother gave me a (chew, few, mew) pennies.

4. Jim (screw, threw, stew) the bag to Tom.

5. We had hot (pew, stew, flew) for our supper.

6. I need a (few, threw, mew) children to help me.

7. You must (flew, chew, grew) your food.

8. The wind (blew, flew, new) the leaves.

9. The baby bird (threw, screw, flew) from his nest.

1. A kitten can (mew, new, blew).

2. Ted (few, drew, grew) a picture of a house.

3. I use my teeth to (new, chew, few).

4. Do you like to (few, new, chew) gum?

5. Who gave that (mew, new, threw) bike to you?

6. The wind (flew, threw, blew) my new hat away.

7. The cat said, "(Pew, New, Mew)."

8. Mother read the (news, pews, chews).

9. Dick (threw, chew, few) it across the street.

DIRECTIONS: Read the sentence, and print a word that fits the meaning of the sentence and contains the two given letters. In the next exercise, see how many words you can complete using only EW, OI, OY, OU, or OW.

Print the word on the line. Use the two letters in the new word.

1. It is a name for money.   oi   _____

2. It is something Mother can cook.   ew   _____

3. It is something a king has.   ow   _____

4. It is something we play with.   oy   _____

5. It is something a kitten says.   ew   _____

6. It means "not in."   ou   _____

7. It is something in the sky.   ou   _____

Print the missing letters in the space.

ew   oi   oy   ou   ow

c_____   c_____nt   cr_____d   c_____n

h_____   h_____se   cl_____n   j_____n

t_____   s_____th   br_____n   b_____s

f_____   n_____se   sh_____t   n_____s

scr_____   p_____nt   sp_____l   b_____l

157

UNIT 8: Review of diphthongs.
DIRECTIONS: Complete each sentence by using a word from the list.

1. The queen wore her _____.

2. Tom _____ his new tin horn.

3. Mary put the _____ in her bank.

4. The farmer has a brown _____.

5. We keep a clean _____ in the kitchen.

6. There was a _____ of people downtown.

7. We may win the game by two _____.

8. Mary is in the _____ next door.

9. Mother told Joe not to _____.

10. Roy is a good _____ at home.

11. Red _____ grow in our yard.

12. The wheel needs a new _____.

13. Mother made me a _____ dress.

14. Dad had _____ put in the car.

15. The _____ did funny tricks.

16. Joan gave Sally a _____.

cow

crowd

new

crown

clown

oil

boy

screw

house

blew

toy

flowers

coin

towel

town

shout

points

Draw a line under the correct word.

1. You use it when you talk.

   spoil   joy   voice   soil

2. It means that something is wet.

   round   join   moist   oil

3. You see him do funny tricks.

   crown   clown   brown   cloud

4. Mother puts it on.

   blouse   mouse   plow   proud

5. It is something you do with gum.

   blew   flew   chew   crew

6. It is something a dog can do.

   howl   join   stew   dew

7. A car needs it.

   joy   boil   oil   plow

8. It is something Baby likes.

   owl   toy   crowd   how

9. It is something we can eat.

   mew   drew   stew   few

10. Mother bakes with it.

    owl   gown   flour   round

11. It means not many.

    new   few   dew   stew

12. It means dirt.

    soil   coil   boy   oil

13. The farmer uses it.

    frown   plow   down   cloud

14. The cat runs after it.

    house   shout   mouse   out

Draw a circle around the <u>ow</u> words.

Just for Fun

"Moo-Moo," said Mother Cow.

"Give me my dinner now."

"Not now, Mother Cow

It is time for me to plow."

DIRECTIONS: Think of a word that will complete the sentence, and at the same time rhyme
with the word that appears behind the sentence. At the bottom of the page,
draw a circle around the OI and OY words.

Find the missing word.

1.   I can hear Billy shout with _____ .   toy

2.   Tim's dog _____ when he is hungry.   owls

3.   All the robins flew _____ .   mouth

4.   The cow _____ the green grass.   pews

5.   Mother Robin _____ from tree to tree.   dew

6.   Our green grass was wet with _____ .   mew

7.   The rain will _____ the picnic.   oil

8.   The boy next door is called _____ .   Toe

9.   Mother needs two cups of _____ .   our

10.   He has a _____ nuts in the bag.   dew

11.   The lemon has a _____ taste.   flour

12.   The _____ is white and fluffy.   loud

Draw a circle around the o̲i̲ and o̲y̲ words.

Roy enjoys toys.

Roy enjoys noise.

So Roy likes the toys

That make a loud noise.

ACROSS:
1. Noises made by kittens
6. Gave food to
9. Must pay
10. Type of paintings
13. Rhymes with food
14. Kind of flower
15. On top of
17. A burro or donkey
18. Everybody
19. By
20. All of us
21. A number
22. Concern or worry
25. Not wet
27. Father
29. Dirties
31. At this time
32. Third note of the musical scale
34. Belonging to us
36. A point on a compass
38. Neither cake __ __ __ candy
40. Tiny
41. Belonging to me
42. Belonging to her

DOWN:
1. A small animal
2. Girl sheep
3. To marry
5. Workers
6. An insect
7. A suffix after CH
11. Sick
12. Go in
13. Cuts wood
14. Ground or soil not in the sea
15. A paddle for rowing
23. Permits
24. Ground covered with grass
26. Contraction for you are
27. A small horse
28. I __ __ big
30. A girl's name
33. Not out
35. Second note of the musical scale
37. A suffix meaning more than one
39. A word that shows surprise

UNIT 8: TEST: Diphthongs.
DIRECTIONS: Complete each sentence with a word from the list.

1. On hot days the meat will _____.   cow

2. My bank is filled with _____.   toy

3. Baby likes her new _____.   spoil

4. Did you hear that _____?   coins

5. The farmer went to milk his _____.   noise

6. The king wore a _____.   sour

7. Bob Brown will sell his brick _____.   house

8. The milk is _____.   crown

---

1. When you jump rope it is fun to _____.   found

2. A car needs gas and _____.   boil

3. Mother wants the water to _____.   stew

4. Dad needs a _____.   oil

5. The boy _____ pie in his lunch box.   count

6. Her coat looks as good as _____.   towel

7. Have you eaten some _____?   south

8. In the winter the birds fly _____.   new

UNIT 9: Consonant digraphs SH, TH, WH, CH, and CK.
DIRECTIONS: Say the name of each picture. Draw a circle around the letters that you hear.

	th sh ck ch wh		th sh ck ch wh		th sh ck ch wh
	th sh ck ch wh		th sh ck ch wh		th sh ck ch wh
	th sh ck ch wh		th sh ck ch wh		th sh ck ch wh
	th sh ck ch wh		th sh ck ch wh		th sh ck ch wh

UNIT 9: Consonant digraphs SH, TH, WH, CH, and CK.
DIRECTIONS: If the consonant digraph is at the beginning of a word, print the word in the first column. If it is in the middle, print the word in the middle column. If it is at the end, print the word in the last column.

cheer	quack	stuck	teeth
reach	peaches	sheep	matches
when	shine	cracked	duck
kicking	peach	dishes	thank
whip	wishing	teaching	splashes
fish	bench	why	chin

BEGINNING	MIDDLE	END

UNIT 9:   Consonant digraphs SH, TH, WH, CH, and CK.
DIRECTIONS: In the first exercise, draw a circle around the word that completes each sentence. At the bottom of the page, print four words containing CH, four containing WH, four containing TH, and four containing SH.

Draw a circle around the missing words.

1. Dick and Joe like to eat	cheese.	sheets.	chase.
2. We played in the sand at the	bunch.	bench.	beach.
3. I can hear the sick puppy	wheel.	white.	whine.
4. Did you brush your	then?	teeth?	there?
5. We went to the pet	shop.	shone.	shame.
6. In my lunch I have a big	reach.	think.	peach.
7. I help Mother with the	shake.	splashes.	dishes.
8. Miss Smith likes to	where.	teach.	chain.

Print the words on the lines.

ch
1 _____
2 _____
3 _____
4 _____

sh
1 _____
2 _____
3 _____
4 _____

wh
1 _____
2 _____
3 _____
4 _____

th
1 _____
2 _____
3 _____
4 _____

Here is a little test.

Do your best.

1.   I hope the sun will (shine, chin).

2.   (Where, There) did you go?

3.   Mother wants us to (thing, think).

4.   I (chose, chair) the big prize.

5.   (This, When) is my best work.

6.   Please get (that, what) glass.

7.   (What, That) time is it?

8.   (They, The) are here.

9.   We will go (when, then) the bell rings.

10.   Did you have (church, chicken) for dinner?

11.   Have you had a ride on a (chip, ship)?

12.   Do not drop that (dish, wish).

13.   Tim likes to play with his (blocks, shocks).

14.   Will you (dish, brush) my suit?

15.   Bill did not (catch, pinch) the ball.

16.   We went to the (chop, shop).

DIRECTIONS: Draw a line from the sentence to the picture it tells about. Then draw a box around all the KN words you can find on this page. See if you can answer the riddles at the bottom of the page.

Draw a box around the kn words.

John has a knot in the rope.

Joan can turn the knob.

Ann has her doll on her knee.

Mother cut it with a knife.

Grandmother likes to knit.

Joe knocks on the door.

Print the answers on the line.

1. Something that is sharp.

2. Something Grandmother did with the yarn.

3. Something that is a part of your leg.

4. Something that is on a door.

5. Something one does before a king.

DIRECTIONS: Find the word that will complete the sentence. At the bottom of the page, see if
   you can think of a KN word that rhymes with each of the words you see.

Find the missing word.

1. I will tie the rope in a_____.   knit   knot

2. Put the_____on the bench.   knife   knit

3. There was a_____at the door.   know   knock

4. Grandmother likes to_____.   knit   knob

5. The door has a shiny brass_____.   knob   knit

6. The boy_____before the king.   kneel   knelt

7. Do you_____the word?   knife   know

8. Jack cut it with his_____.   knit   knife

9. Bob fell and hurt his_____.   knee   knob

Print a kn word that rhymes.

snow	sit	feel
block	wife	blew
cob	see	hot

UNIT 9: Ending LE.
DIRECTIONS: Print the correct word below each picture.

apple	eagle	needle	people
candle	turtle	handle	thimble
steeple	marble	puzzle	bubbles

UNIT 9:   Ending LE.
DIRECTIONS: Find the correct word, and complete the sentence.

1. The baby has a _____ in each cheek.   purple

2. Red and blue make _____.   dimple

3. Will you try to guess my _____?   sample

4. Please let us _____ the cake.   riddle

5. The _____ fell off the tree.   handle

6. The _____ of the hammer is made of wood.   apple

7. Jack tried to jump over the _____ but fell in.   pickle

8. The dill _____ made my mouth water.   puddle

---

1. The _____ is boiling on the stove.   rattle

2. Please try not to _____ when I cut your hair.   kettle

3. I lit the _____ on the cake   candles

4. The baby played with his _____.   wiggle

5. The church bells were hung in the _____.   fiddle

6. The _____ is the king of birds.   turtle

7. The cat played the _____ and sang.   steeple

8. The _____ can go into its shell.   eagle

UNIT 9: Consonant digraph WR.
DIRECTIONS: Complete the sentences using words from the list.

| wrap | wren | write |

wrote   wreck   wrong   write   wrench

wren   wreath   wrap   wrist   wrestle

1. Please_____your name on the line.

2. There is a_____in the window.

3. Five of my spelling words were_____.

4. Who_____that letter to you?

5. Two new cars were in a_____.

6. The_____sat on her eggs.

7. When Jean fell she broke her_____.

8. Mr. Jones fixed the car with his_____.

9. Sue can_____a letter to her friend.

10. The green_____looked pretty on the door.

11. Most boys like to_____.

DIRECTIONS: Print the answers to the riddles on the blackboard. You will find the answers listed below.

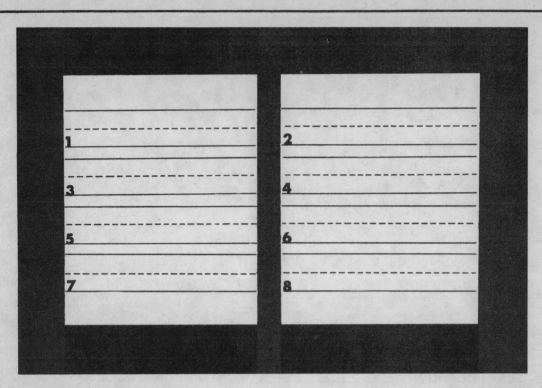

wren   wrench   wrecker   wreath   wrapper   writer   wrist   typewriter

1. I am round and green.
   I am put on the door.
   What am I?

2. I am made of paper.
   I keep candy clean.
   What am I called?

3. I am a little bird.
   I like to sing.
   What is my name?

4. I am a useful tool.
   I can fix things.
   What is my name?

5. I am part of the arm.
   I can twist and turn.
   What am I called?

6. I can write.
   People punch my keys.
   What is my name?

7. I am a big truck.
   I tow away cars.
   What am I called?

8. I am one who writes.
   I make up stories.
   What am I called?

UNIT 9: Consonant digraphs KN and WR.
DIRECTIONS: Complete the sentences using words from the list.

knows	wrapped	knock
wrong	kneel	wrote
written	knitted	doorknob
shipwreck	jackknife	wring

1. We had to _____ out our wet suits.

2. Ann _____ some red and white socks with silk yarn.

3. The clerk _____ the gift in dark blue paper.

4. Mary _____ her spelling words.

5. Did you _____ at the front door?

6. Please _____ down and tie your shoe.

7. The _____ was shown on TV.

8. Each of the scouts had a _____ .

9. Your work is neatly _____ .

10. The _____ is made of brass.

11. It is _____ to tell a lie.

12. Sally _____ a letter from camp.

DIRECTIONS: Say the name of each picture. Where do you hear the consonant digraph; at the beginning, middle, or end? Print the consonant digraph in the correct block.

wh	ch	th

wr	sh	ck

w	sh	kn

UNIT 9: TEST: Consonant digraphs.
DIRECTIONS: Read each sentence. Find the answer in the column at the right, and print the number of the answer in the space.

It is something we can eat.	_____	1. sheet
Mother puts it on your bed.	_____	2. knee
You can sit on it.	_____	3. jungle
It is part of your leg.	_____	4. chair
Lions are in this place.	_____	5. peach

It is wrong to do this.	_____	1. teeth
An auto runs on them.	_____	2. rinkle
We slice bread with this.	_____	3. wheels
We must brush them every day.	_____	4. chea
Sometimes we do this to our paper.	_____	5. knife

It is part of my finger.	_____	1. wheat
The baker makes bread from this.	_____	2. peaches
They are red and yellow and grow on trees.	_____	3. knuckle
I had one in my shoelace.	_____	4. wreath
You hang it in your window.	_____	5. knot

UNIT 10:   Prefix RE-.

DIRECTIONS: Print RE in front of each word in the list to make a new word. Then complete the sentences using the new words.

When the prefix RE is used the meaning of the word changes. It means to do again.

reread

The prefix is re-.

The root word is read.

_____ plant   _____ write   _____ wrap   _____ pack

_____ pay   _____ read   _____ load   _____ heat

_____ make   _____ tell   _____ spell   _____ paint

1. Take this clean paper and _____ your letter.

2. Ann wants to _____ this book to her mother.

3. Mark will _____ all the words for us.

4. Mother will _____ the beds.

5. The cowboy has to _____ his gun.

6. The farmer must _____ his corn patch.

7. Grandfather is going to _____ his trunk.

8. Now you may _____ the package.

9. Dad is going to _____ Dick's bedroom.

10. Joe will _____ the joke.

UNIT 10: Prefix UN-.
DIRECTIONS: In the list of words, print UN before each word and then use the new words to complete the sentences.

When the prefix UN is placed before some words, the meaning of the word is changed to mean just the opposite.

unhappy

The prefix is un–.

The root word is happy.

This puppy is happy.   This puppy is unhappy.

_____ safe   _____ lock   _____ happy   _____ fair

_____ opened   _____ selfish   _____ paid   _____ cooked

_____ tie   _____ dress   _____ clean   _____ fold

1. I will_____my doll and put her to bed.

2. Ann was_____and shared her candy.

3. Tom had to_____the gym floor.

4. When Jack broke his toy he was_____.

5. I will_____the knot in the string.

6. It is_____to cheat in a game.

7. The gifts lay _____ on the desk.

8. Do not eat with_____hands.

9. One box was marked "_____Bills."

UNIT 10:   Prefixes RE- and UN-.
DIRECTIONS: Complete the sentences by using the word at the side, and adding the prefix RE or
UN to the word. At the bottom of the page, make a new word that means the
same thing as the two words you see.

Use re and un.

1. read   Please _____ the book.

2. opened   Your letter is _____ .

3. make   Ann will _____ the beds.

4. heat   Mother wants to _____ the soup.

5. happy   Tom was _____ about going away.

6. dress   Jean wants to _____ the baby.

7. write   Dick will _____ his homework.

8. fair   It is _____ to cheat.

9. plant   The man wants to _____ the grass.

10. paint   Joe will _____ his old car.

11. paid   The poor man's bill was _____ .

Print the one word that means the same.

not cooked   _____   spell again   _____

not clean   _____   read again   _____

not safe   _____   use again   _____

not selfish   _____   pack again   _____

UNIT 10:   Prefix DIS-.
DIRECTIONS: Make new words by printing DIS in front of the words in the list. Use the new words to complete the sentences.

disobey

The prefix is dis–.
The root word is obey.

_____ agree   _____ colors   _____ pleased

_____ connect   _____ trust   _____ like

_____ obey   _____ honest   _____ order

1.   Jean's mother was _____ with her work.

2.   One who steals is _____.

3.   The lunchroom was in _____.

4.   It is wrong to _____ the law.

5.   I _____ getting up in the morning.

6.   Miss Gray was _____ with my printing.

7.   I _____ with what Ann said.

8.   We had to _____ the wires.

9.   The sun _____ my blue hat.

10.   If you steal, people will _____ you.

DIRECTIONS: Print RE, UN, or DIS, before the root word to make a new word. In the exercise below, add a prefix to the underlined word to make the sentence have an opposite meaning, and print the new sentence on the line.

un– or dis–

_____ please   _____ agree

_____ kind   _____ obey

_____ order   _____ fair

_____ easy   _____ color

Use <u>un</u> or <u>dis</u> before the word that is underlined to make the sentence have an opposite meaning. Print the new sentence on the line.

1. <u>Lock</u> the door.

2. <u>Wrap</u> the box.

3. Did Sue <u>obey</u>?

4. <u>Tie</u> the bow.

5. I <u>like</u> the book.

6. Did he <u>please</u> Mother?

7. Do you <u>agree</u>?

8. <u>Pack</u> the basket.

9. <u>Load</u> the truck.

UNIT 10:   TEST: Prefixes RE-, UN-, and DIS-.
DIRECTIONS: Find the correct prefix. Draw a circle around it, and print it on the line.

1. Ann will _____ check her paper.   re   d

2. Father _____ painted the house.   un

3. The books on the shelf are in _____ order.   dis   e

4. Mother will _____ wrap the package.   dis   un

5. Did you _____ read the story yet?   un   re

6. My mother _____ likes riding in trains.   re   dis

7. The ice is _____ safe for skating.   u   re

8. Do you have to _____ write the words?   is   re

9. The top of Jim's paper is _____ even.   re   un

10. A boy is _____ liked if he is bad.   re   dis

11. Father will _____ lock the back door.   un   dis

12. I hurt my mother when I _____ obey her.   dis   re

13. Bob helped Mother _____ plant the flowers.   un   re

14. Nancy is an _____ selfish girl.   re   un

15. Will you please _____ fold this paper?   re   dis

16. The ink will _____ color the white dress.   un   dis

DIRECTIONS: Find a word under the picture that means the same or almost the same as a word in the list, and print it on the line. Then draw a box around the word in each row at the bottom that means the same or almost the same as the first word in each row.

Print the words on the lines.

Be a Good Thinker!

shut	
sad	
big	
happy	
sick	
small	
stone	
auto	
quick	

glad   car   unhappy   fast
rock   little   ill   large   close

Draw a box around the words that mean the same or almost the same.

1.	jolly	sad	big	happy	jump
2.	clean	slow	funny	unsoiled	big
3.	pile	heap	near	rest	stop
4.	sleep	awake	nap	paint	read
5.	hurt	far	happy	sad	harm
6.	sick	ill	quick	lazy	glad
7.	quick	step	slow	pony	fast

UNIT 11: Antonyms.

DIRECTIONS: Think of a word that is of opposite meaning to a word in the list, and print it on the line. The words at the bottom of the page will help you.

dry	_____	up	_____
summer	_____	short	_____
near	_____	fast	_____
clean	_____	bad	_____
cold	_____	thin	_____
sick	_____	little	_____
yes	_____	black	_____
first	_____	on	_____
new	_____	open	_____
in	_____	asleep	_____

old	wet	no	slow
last	down	hot	good
dirty	out	well	big
winter	long	far	white
off	shut	awake	fat

a little fish

a big fish

UNIT 11:   Synonyms and antonyms.

DIRECTIONS: In the first exercise, draw a line between the two words having the same or almost the same meaning. In the second exercise, if the two words have the same or almost the same meaning, print an S in the space. If they are of opposite meaning, print an O.

Draw a line between the two words.

lad	big	cure	sick
large	unhappy	ill	bigger
sad	boy	larger	close
glad	stay	rock	heal
quick	happy	auto	stone
remain	fast	shut	car

Print S or O in the space between the two words.

first	_____ last	stop	_____ go	small	_____ wee
little	_____ small	quick	_____ slow	happy	_____ sad
yes	_____ no	come	_____ go	work	_____ play
in	_____ out	top	_____ bottom	float	_____ sink
fast	_____ slow	unhappy	_____ sad	loud	_____ noisy
quick	_____ fast	auto	_____ car	hot	_____ cold
under	_____ over	bad	_____ good	sick	_____ ill
hard	_____ soft	glad	_____ happy	sweet	_____ bitter
up	_____ down	long	_____ short	white	_____ black

UNIT 11: TEST: Synonyms and antonyms.
DIRECTIONS: In the first exercise, draw a line under the two words in each box that have the same or almost the same meaning. In the second exercise, draw a line between the two words in each box that have opposite meanings.

Draw a line under each of the two words which have the same meaning.

unhappy	sad	big	green	brick	happy
door	barn	large	sky	just	glad
steal	rob	hair	small	fast	fell
seed	shook	little	home	quick	queen
three	tree	lift	raise	kick	snow
jolly	happy	drink	drop	ill	blow
look	fish	smile	go	place	thin
see	first	start	top	slim	play

Draw a line between the two words which have the opposite meaning.

little	puppy	fly	fat	up	candy
Billy	big	thin	penny	down	good
they	fast	from	dirty	asleep	play
play	slow	clean	funny	baby	awake
take	turkey	out	in	door	chair
day	give	sleep	try	shut	open
bad	stood	wing	go	cold	fairy
come	good	come	wind	hot	spring

185

UNIT 11:   Homonyms.
DIRECTIONS: In the first exercise, find a word in the list at the top of the page that sounds the same as a word in the exercise, and print it on the line. In the second exercise, complete each sentence by printing the correct word on the line.

Find the words that sound the same.

here	road	pear	son	tail	sail	pain
to	reel	pail	so	week	maid	sea
meet	plain	beet	heal	cent	deer	blue

heel _____

rode _____

blew _____

hear _____

sale _____

meat _____

plane _____

beat _____

sent _____

weak _____

two _____

made _____

pane _____

pair _____

see _____

tale _____

pale _____

sow _____

sun _____

real _____

dear _____

Find the missing words. _____

1. Can you _____ the bell?   hear   here

2. I _____ a funny clown.   see   sea

3. Our puppy wagged his _____ .   tale   tail

4. The _____ hid in the woods.   deer   dear

5. The boat has a big white _____ .   sale   sail

6. The _____ is round and hot.   son   sun

186

UNIT 11: Homonyms.
DIRECTIONS: Find the pairs of words that sound alike, and print them on the lines. Then from this list choose the correct words that complete the sentences at the bottom of the page.

Print the two words.

hear	pale	sun	weak	sent	blue
son	blew	week	beat	dear	to
heal	two	heel	here	pain	see
tale	pane	rode	meet	cent	sea
meat	pail	tail	beet	road	dear

Print the missing words in the spaces.

1. I paid one_____for the candy.

2. I gave her_____of my story books.

3. Mother can_____the baby singing.

4. The_____was shining in my window.

5. Grandmother_____me a letter.

6. The sky is very_____today.

UNIT 11: TEST: Homonyms.

DIRECTIONS: Draw a line under the correct word, and print it on the line. In the exercise at the bottom of the page, draw a line between the two words that sound alike.

Find the missing words.

1. Mother made me a _____ dress.   read   red

2. He did not _____ Bill's dime.   steal   steel

3. Will you _____ me in school?   meet   meat

4. She broke the window _____.   pain   pane

5. The store is having a _____.   sail   sale

6. A ship is sailing on the _____.   see   sea

7. Dad feels _____ today.   week   weak

8. Your _____ dress is nice.   blew   blue

Draw a line between the two words that sound alike.

sun	maid	tail	week	red	pair
seem	son	pale	pail	pear	read
made	seam	weak	tale	beat	beet

pane	pain	two	deer	so	rode
in	blew	heel	too	road	here
blue	inn	dear	heal	hear	sow

188

DIRECTIONS: Read each sentence, and print the phrase that answers the question on the lines
            below.

1. Mother asked me to get sliced bread.

2. The flag hung on the big stage.

3. The large candy bar was too hard to eat.

4. Mark burned his fingers on the hot corn.

5. Mother got a fur coat for her birthday.

6. "Chirp! Chirp! Chirp!" sang the perky little bird.

7. Take your place in the circle.

8. Bruce put the mice in a huge cage.

1. What did Mother ask me to get? _____

2. Where did the flag hang? _____

3. What was too hard to eat? _____

4. On what did Mark burn his fingers? _____

5. What did Mother get for her birthday? _____

6. Who sang "Chirp! Chirp! Chirp?" _____

7. Where should you take your place? _____

8. Where did Bruce put the mice? _____

DIRECTIONS: Read each sentence, and print the phrase that answers the question on the lines below.

1. Mother is filling two boxes with peaches.

2. Jack played with the baby puppies.

3. The spicecake was served with whipped cream.

4. Tom dropped the armful of pine branches he was carrying.

5. Don't ask Peggy why she isn't reading.

6. Stop saying, "I can't." Say, "I'll try!"

7. Mother doesn't know that the milkman didn't come.

8. She's trying to tell you that it's fun.

1. What is Mother filling?

2. With what was Jack playing?

3. How was the spicecake served?

4. What did Tom drop?

5. What must you not ask Peggy?

6. What should you say?

7. What doesn't Mother know?

8. What is she trying to tell you?

1. Joy gave her mother a lace doily for her birthday.

2. The spoiled boy played with his sister's toys.

3. When men are unjust, they are unhappy.

4. The crowds clapped as the silly clown bowed.

5. The witch with a crooked nose rode a broomstick.

6. "Shoo, Moo Cow. Shoo!" cried the little girl.

7. Jean wore the leather belt with her sweater.

8. The squaw had drawn the red shawl close to her.

1. What did Joy give her mother?

2. Who played with his sister's toys?

3. When men are unjust, what happens?

4. Who did the bowing?

5. What kind of a nose did the witch have?

6. What did the little girl cry to the cow?

7. What did Jean wear with her sweater?

8. What did the squaw draw close to her?

DEFINITIONS AND RULES

The **vowels** are *a, i, u, o, e,* and sometimes **y** and **w**.

The **consonants** are the remaining letters.

A **consonant blend** consists of two or more consonants sounded together in such a way that each is heard——*black, train, cry, swim, spring.*

A **consonant digraph** consists of two consonants that together represent one sound——*when, thin, this, church, sheep, pack, know, write.*

An **irregular double vowel** is a double vowel that does not follow Long Vowel Rule I——*school, book, bread, auto, yawn.*

A **diphthong** consists of two vowels blended together to form a compound speech sound——*cloud, boy, oil, new.*

Short Vowel Rule: If a word (or syllable) has only one vowel and it comes at the beginning or between two consonants, the vowel is usually short——*am, is, bag, fox.*

Long Vowel Rule I: If a one-part word (or syllable) has two vowels, the first vowel is usually long and the second is silent—*rain, kite, cane, jeep.*

Long Vowel Rule II: If a word (or syllable) has one vowel and it comes at the end of the word (or syllable), the vowel is usually long—*we, go, cupid, pony.*

Y As a Vowel Rule:
1) If **Y** is the only vowel at the end of a one-syllable word, **Y** has the sound of long I—*fly, try, by.*
2) If **Y** is the only vowel at the end of a word of more than one syllable, **Y** has a sound almost like long **E**—*silly, funny, baby.*

Soft C and G Rule: When *c* and *g* are followed by *e, i,* or *y,* they are usually soft——*ice, city, change, gym.*